RESISTANCE

Other Books by Jules Archer

African Firebrand: Kenyatta of Kenya
Angry Abolitionist: William Lloyd Garrison
Battlefield President: Dwight D. Eisenhower
Chou En-lai
Colossus of Europe: Metternich
Congo
The Dictators
The Executive "Success"
The Extremists: Gadflies of American Society
Famous Young Rebels
Fighting Journalist: Horace Greeley
Front-Line General: Douglas MacArthur
Hawks, Doves, and the Eagle
Ho Chi Minh: The Legend of Hanoi
Indian Foe, Indian Friend
Laws That Changed America
Man of Steel: Joseph Stalin
Mao Tse-tung: A Biography
Mexico and The United States
1968: Year of Crisis
Philippines' Fight for Freedom
The Plot to Seize the White House
Red Rebel: Tito of Yugoslavia
Revolution in Our Time
Science Explorer: Roy Chapman Andrews
Strikes, Bombs, and Bullets: Big Bill Haywood and the I.W.W.
Thorn in Our Flesh: Castro's Cuba
They Made A Revolution: 1776
Treason in America: Disloyalty versus Dissent
Twentieth-century Caesar: Benito Mussolini
Uneasy Friendship: France and the United States
The Unpopular Ones
World Citizen: Woodrow Wilson

RESISTANCE

By
Jules Archer

MACRAE SMITH COMPANY
Philadelphia

Library of Congress Catalog Card Number 73-13628

Manufactured in the United States of America

Published simultaneously in Canada by
George J. McLeod, Limited, Toronto

7310

Library of Congress Cataloging in Publication Data

Archer, Jules.
  Resistance.

  Bibliography: p.
  1. Government, Resistance to. I. Title.
JC328.3.A73   322.4'4   73-13628
ISBN 0-8255-1300-6

Excerpts from *Lithopinion* reprinted by permission from *Lithopinion*
No. 11, the graphic arts and public affairs journal of Local One, Amal-
gamated Lithographers of America (New York) and by Victor Borge.
©1968 by Local One, A.L.A.

To
Kerry Russell Archer,
at Tufts University School of Medicine,
and Jan Archer
with love.

Contents

RESISTANCE

I Why Do People
Resist the Law?

Suzi Williams of Amherst, Massachusetts, was seventeen in 1966 when she joined the Committee for Nonviolent Action in protest against the Vietnam War she considered a crime against humanity. Inspired by Mahatma Gandhi's principles of civil disobedience, she sought to disrupt the launching of the first nuclear submarine by handing out leaflets of protest at the shipyard gate on the day of the official ceremony.

Ordered to leave, she sat down on the ground instead. Arresting police had to carry her off because she went limp and refused to walk or cooperate in any way with her arrest. Her clothes were torn as she was dragged roughly up three flights of stairs in a New London, Connecticut, courthouse. Bruised, Suzi apologized to the police for inconveniencing them.

She refused to stand up in the courtroom for her arraignment. When the judge angrily demanded that she show respect to the court, Suzi replied quietly, "I don't in good conscience feel that I can cooperate with this court." The judge sentenced her to thirty days in jail for "criminal contempt."

So the girl who did not drink, smoke, swear or use narcotics, an honor student and Girl Scout counselor, winner of a Daughters of the American Revolution award for good citizenship, was dragged off to serve time with junkies, thieves, prostitutes and other women with criminal records.

Behind bars Suzi went on a four-day fast to mourn anniversaries of the atomic bombings of Hiroshima and Nagasaki.

When her sentence was up, she was brought before another judge to stand trial on the original charges. Again she refused to cooperate and had to be dragged into court, where she was dropped on the floor in front of the judge's bench.

Asked why she was being so stubborn, Suzi explained, "To assist in my punishment for taking a stand against war is wrong, so I noncooperate. To be told I must pay respect to a court whose actions I consider wrong requires my noncooperation."

The baffled judge sentenced her to two more months in jail on new "contempt" charges and warned, "I'm sure my successor will keep meting it [punishment] out until you conform. You just cannot come in here and tell the court how to operate."

Suzi began a new 10-day fast on water, in imitation of her idol, Gandhi. Her worried father wrote a letter to the Hartford *Courant* protesting, "Suzanne is not looking for mercy, only justice. She is a political prisoner and is being treated more harshly than are prisoners of war under the provisions of the Geneva convention."

Once the public became aware of Suzi's case, her treatment inspired popular indignation. A protest march demanded her freedom. Pacifists staged round-the-clock vigils and fasts in front of the jail. The American Civil Liberties Union fought for her release. Suzi firmly refused to apologize to the court, consenting only to sign a statement affirming that her resistance was for a principle and was not intended to indicate disrespect for American justice.

After her sixty-eighth day in jail, the second judge who had sentenced her ordered all charges dropped, and Suzi went home.

. There are many different reasons why people feel driven to resist the law, reasons just as compelling as those which drove a deeply motivated pacifist like Suzi Williams.

Resistance is often sparked when strongly individualistic citizens feel "pushed around" by government bureaucracy. New York State, wanting to build a superhighway, forced the sale of a group of houses that stood in the way. One elderly woman who had lived on the spot all her life refused to sell or leave. Planting herself in a porch rocking chair, a rifle across her lap, she threatened to shoot the first law officer who "trespassed" and tried to remove her from her home.

Resistance is often a response to persecution as a group.

Frequently it is inspired by abhorrence of an evil act or acts by one's own government. Popular folk singer Joan Baez, protesting atrocities committed by U.S. forces in Vietnam, resisted paying her taxes. Her attempt to withhold the portion that went into the military budget made headlines that widely advertised her reasons for dissent.

Citizens who fear further industrial expansion as a threat to their way of life are increasingly impelled to resist it. New York State officials were startled recently when plans to build a new jet airport at Newburgh and a new power plant on the Hudson were resolutely thwarted by citizens. Committees from those areas quickly organized to stop the projects as pollution menaces.

Constant violation of one's basic rights as a citizen is another major reason for discontent that leads to resistance. On December 4, 1955, a quiet black woman named Mrs. Rosa Parks boarded a Montgomery, Alabama, bus and found that all of the seats in the "black section" were filled. Tired from work, fed up with a lifetime of segregation, she sat down in the "white section" and refused to move to the rear of the bus when ordered.

Her simple act of resistance, followed by her arrest and imprisonment, led to the Montgomery bus boycott headed by Martin Luther King that sparked escalation of the black protest movement for the next fifteen years.

Establishment decrees that violate the intellectual convictions of individuals may inspire resistance. Two Queens, New York, twelve-year-olds, Susan Keller and Mary Frain, refused to join in or stand for the recitation of the Pledge of Allegiance recited each morning at Junior High School 217. The Pledge, they insisted, was hypocritical. "Liberty and justice for all?" Mary said. "That's not true for the blacks and poor whites." Susan also objected to the words "under God," because she did not believe in a deity. Both refused to yield to pressure and were suspended from school.

Powerfully held political beliefs may gestate heroic acts of resistance. Lady Amalia Fleming, Greek wife of the British discoverer of penicillin, enraged the military junta that rules Greece by helping a young Greek partisan escape from prison. Arrested and jailed herself, she was alternately threatened with torture and offered a cabinet post if she would endorse the dictatorship. Defying her captors, she was finally deported from Greece as an embarrassment to the tyrannical regime.

Resistance can be expected from groups or movements with principles diametrically opposed to those of a President, king, dictator or system of government. In 1963 Vietnamese Buddhists burned themselves alive to protest the Catholic regime of Ngo Dinh Diem, which represented only ten percent of South Vietnam's people. Quakers have always resisted fighting for any government that goes to war. The Dukhobors of Canada, sworn to defy any authority but that of their clan leader, have often gone to jail rather than obey government orders.

Workers express their resistance to unfair pay, benefits or conditions in union strikes or slowdowns. Most public service workers—teachers, firemen, policemen, post office employees and government clerks—are forbidden by law to strike. But today they often defy these laws, as well as court injunctions, going to jail to defend their right to do so.

Most individuals who join a resistance movement are motivated by a desire for justice, but there are exceptions. One is the person who is not deeply committed to a cause but joins it to advance his own political or monetary fortunes. Another is the paid agent of a foreign power whose mission is to create turmoil or rebellion. A third is the *agent provocateur*, a government agent paid to infiltrate the resistance movement, betray its leaders and destroy it.

There are two basic reasons for most forms of resistance. One is personal resentment of laws the individual considers wrong or unjust because they affect him unfavorably. The other is the outrage a citizen feels on behalf of others he considers unjustly treated by the government, in violation of the letter or spirit of the law or of the humane traditions he believes his country stands for.

Ever since Mahatma Gandhi showed the way in India, resistance has been considered the most civilized way to oppose tyranny in any country where the normal channels of change fail to function because grievances are ignored. It functions best when most of the citizenry feel oppressed and united in their opposition, as Indians were against the British.

The task of resisters is much more difficult when they are in the minority, however. Like the crowds in the fable, the majority is often brainwashed into agreeing with the King's advisors, who assure him that he is clad in brilliant raiment. There is consternation when a tiny voice shrills the plain truth: "The King is naked!" It is usually the minority that punctures the myth of government respectability by exposing its pretensions and hypocrisies.

"The hue and cry for law and order is a typical American sham," William L. Akers, a black Philadelphia attorney, wrote bitterly in the Spring of 1970. "The call is sounded loudest by a Congress still finding Indian treaties to break; by a President conducting a war without constitutional sanction; by City Halls riddled with scandalous misappropriation of public funds; by Police Departments that resort to assassination while deploring violence, and by a whole nation continually in violation of the Thirteenth and Fourteenth Amendments."

Resistance increases when a government creates distrust by lying or suppressing the truth. In a 1969 commencement address called "The Necessity for the Cultural Revolution in the United States," Brown University graduate Ira Charles Magaziner cited a long list of lies he charged the government with telling, leading to his disillusionment.

"This was further substantiated," he said, "by my believing the United States government when it said for many years that it was not bombing in Laos during the Vietnam War, and then for it finally to admit that it was and had been doing so for three and a half years, while denying it for that amount of time. Just recently another example were those sheep that were killed in Utah. The Army kept denying for a long time that it had anything to do with the nerve-gas plant that they happen to have in the area, until finally it came out a few weeks ago in some Senate testimony. This has created quite a bit of a credibility gap which makes it really impossible to believe or trust the government."

Television has had a great deal to do with the spread of resistance in our time by bringing live pictures of official acts of violence—by soldiers and police—into our homes.

"This is not fiction," Gunnar Myrdal, director of the Institute of International Economic Studies in Stockholm, pointed out in 1968. "Real people are killed. We see them lying dead . . . . The effect is that youth discovers the credibility gap. It sees the horrible reality of the war. It feels that it is being talked to by liars. To young people this is serious. This is what has roused the generation. This is what has given us the present period of protests and demonstrations."

A society's selective morality also breeds resistance. Youth is angered when police club down police or civil rights pickets but do nothing to stop hard-hats who attack the demonstrators. Or when white businessmen found guilty of corporate fraud are merely fined, while poor blacks who commit minor misdemeanors go to jail. Or when the White House demands an $81 billion military budget in peacetime while slashing funds for education, the poor, the handicapped and the aged.

"There is a limit at which forbearance ceases to be a virtue," said Thomas Burke. Many middle-class youths are in rebellion against the society in which they were raised, judging its failings harshly. They accuse Middle America of obsession with material possessions, indifference to pollution of the environment, insensitivity to the needs of the underprivileged, racism, encouragement of police brutality, intolerance of dissent, selective morality about alcohol and marijuana, emphasis on appearances rather than values, and mindless conformism.

The college youth of today, more thoughtful than his elders, more uncompromising in his search for a meaningful life style, is often accused of ingratitude for the opportunities given him by the society he rejects. But he cannot forget the thousands of young people who were killed or crippled in a widely hated war, or the thousands who were brutalized for protesting it, or forced into prison or exile.

"He sees the system for what it is," observed Professor Jerome S. Sloan of Temple University Law School in 1970, "an organized form of violence allowing him limited participation until it asks him to lay down his life. Is it any wonder that he is skeptical, cynical, suspicious, hostile? Is it any wonder that he regards most of his elders as hypocrites?"

In June, 1969, a Gallup Poll survey revealed that students on most campuses were convinced "that society as a whole is seriously ill and that changes are imperative." A Roper poll that year also found forty percent of college seniors "pessimistic to some degree about the direction American society is taking." Two years later campus alienation had become so profound that in a 1971 survey of over 1,200 students on fifty campuses by Daniel Yankelovich, Inc., thirty percent declared they would rather live in some other country than the United States.

Resistance has a special appeal for participants in that it breeds a unique bond of companionship, of common high purpose, that is exhilarating. One gathers spiritual strength by becoming part of a crusade against injustice.

"No one is quite the same after he has marched in a demonstration, however tame," observed Andrew Kopkind in *The New York Times Magazine.*

Harvard student David Goldring recalled his first antiwar march on Washington: "When we got up on the Capitol steps I looked back, and all the way to where the road dipped before the monument was solid with people. Oh, man, was that exciting! I was just delirious! More than ever before, I got the direct physical knowledge of a movement we were all part of. It was just a grand day!"

"Any group act of civil disobedience," states Charles A. Reich in *The Greening of America,* "creates an intense feeling of togetherness. Students who lived in the occupied buildings at Columbia during the 1968 events reported that the communal experience was like nothing else they had known in their entire lives; they returned only with regret to more ordinary ways of living."

Some individuals join or organize resistance movements because they are "natural-born rebels," nonconformists who cannot abide or accept the restraints of authority. In some cases they are young people in rebellion against their parents, transferring their alienation to the society.

Often, however, they are the children of parents who support resistance.

Anarchists are "natural-born rebels," who refuse to submit to the dictates of any government because they believe that the individual has the right to be free of all rulers. So are many cynics and skeptics who agree with Lord Acton's premise, "Power corrupts, and absolute power corrupts absolutely."

I once asked a brilliant American Socialist who had spent his whole life in resistance against the capitalist system whether he would miss the struggle if the United States ever went Socialist. "No," he replied, "because the new government would probably become just as corrupt, and I'd go on fighting *it*."

There is never any shortage of injustices to resist.

"The only thing I love about liberty is the struggle for it," wrote Norway's famous playwright, Henrik Ibsen. "I care nothing for the possession of it . . . . He who possesses liberty as something already achieved possesses it dead and soulless; for the essence of the idea of liberty is that it continue to develop steadily as men pursue it and make it part of their being. Anyone who stops in the middle of the struggle and says, 'Now I have it,' shows that he has lost it."

In recent times normally timid people have not hesitated to join resistance movements because, ironically, participation has become fashionably prestigious instead of stigmatic.

" 'Civil disobedience'—a euphemism for breaking those laws in which the lawbreaker does not believe—has become both respectable and relatively safe," complained *Newsweek's* Stewart Alsop in July 1971. "The civil rights movement of the early '60s began to make it respectable, and the increasing unpopularity of the Vietnam war has helped to make it safe."

We need to know more about the powerful force of nonviolent resistance, at home and around the world. It is obviously going to play an increasingly important role in the lives of all of us. Leading resistance movements since World War II are examined in the following pages, analyzing how and why some succeeded while others failed.

This book also explores the significance resistance can have in our own personal everyday lives—where and how it might be used intelligently as a peaceful catalyst to bring about desirable changes that will make our lives freer and happier, our relationships healthier, our country a finer and more just place for all of us to live in.

2 Is Resistance Un-American?

Our own past teaches us that when grievances held by a substantial number of citizens are ignored, resistance is the traditional American reaction. John Adams declared that the American Revolution had begun not in 1776 but long before, with the resistance "in the Minds and Hearts of the People."

"The People of America," he wrote, "had been educated in an habitual affection for England as their Mother-Country . . . . But when they found her a cruel Beldam, willing, like Lady Macbeth, to 'dash their brains out,' it is no wonder if their filial Affections . . . changed into Indignation and horror. This radical Change in the Principles, Opinions, Sentiments and Affections of the People, was the real American Revolution."

Their resistance was fueled by Thomas Paine's inflammatory tract *Common Sense*, which asked, "Hath your house been burnt? Hath your property been destroyed before your face? Are your wife and children destitute of a bed to lie on, or bread to live on? Have you lost a parent or a child by [British] hands, and yourself the ruined and wretched survivor? If you have not, then are you not a judge of those who have? But if you have, and still can shake hands with the murderers, then you are unworthy the name of husband, father, friend, or lover, and whatever may be your rank or title in life, you have the heart of a coward, and the spirit of a sycophant."

Before July 4, 1776, the Americans who defied British troops were not revolutionists but resisters, with no flag or nation of their own. They were fighting simply for their rights as Englishmen. Only when they were denied those rights did they formulate a Declaration of Independence based on the views of British philosopher John Locke.

Locke held that if a sovereign demands obedience to a decree the individual considers unlawful, the individual is not obliged to obey that law against his conscience. He is not the rebel in such a case, Locke insisted, but the ruler who assumes powers that are not legally his to take.

Significantly, when George III resolved on war against his resisting colonies, no less than nineteen of his lords signed a solemn protest against it, and his two highest military commanders, Lord Jeffrey Amherst and Admiral Keppel, refused to serve in what they branded as an unjust war.

Had the British majority been more responsive to the grievances of its American cousins, a bloody revolution would have been averted, and eventually Americans would have gained their independence peacefully within the British Commonwealth, like Canadians and Australians.

There is nothing un-American about resisting the right of the majority to impose its will on dissenting minorities. President James Madison strongly distrusted majority power.

"It is of great importance in a republic not only to guard the society against the oppression of its rulers," he wrote in *The Federalist*, "but to guard one part of the society against the injustice of the other part . . . . In a society under the forms of which the stronger faction can readily unite and oppress the weaker, anarchy may as truly be said to reign as in a state of nature where the weaker individual is not secured against the violence of the stronger."

Tyranny of the majority can be as oppressive as any other kind of tyranny, driving its victims to desperate measures of resistance. The Declaration of Independence proclaims " . . . that whenever any form of government becomes destructive of these ends, it is the right of the people to alter or to abolish it, and to institute new governments . . . ."

Thomas Jefferson had faith in the justice of majority rule, yet did not hesitate upon becoming President to nullify the pernicious Alien and Sedition Acts which a majority of Americans under President John Adams had sanctioned to punish dissenters. "People are not easily disposed to right themselves," Jefferson admitted, "by abolishing the forms to which they are accustomed."

That early analyst of American democracy, astute Alexis de Tocqueville, admired the system but considered it flawed by what he characterized "tyranny by the majority." The intolerance of the majority was still apparent 130 years later in a Harris Poll survey made in September 1965.

It revealed, "The man who stands apart from the crowd—because he does not believe in God, because he pickets against the war in Vietnam, because he demonstrates for civil rights—is regarded as harmful to the American way of life by two out of three of his fellow citizens."

The Reverend William Sloane Coffin, Jr., the Yale chaplain whose advocacy of draft resistance led to his arrest and trial, declared, "As men frequently vote their ignorance, fears and prejudices, there is never a guarantee that majority rule represents the rule of conscience."

The majority is often less concerned with the issues raised by dissenters than with a feared threat to law and order. But most resisters—students, anti-war demonstrators, blacks, the poor, environmentalists, hippies, women's lib groups, strikers—seek to avoid violence, well aware that in any conflict with police or troops they are bound to get the worst of it.

If the authorities are determined to suppress a demonstration by bayonet or nightstick, however, resisters are then faced with only three choices—flight, fight or jail.

An early case in point was America's Whiskey Rebellion of 1794, when the government imposed a ruinous tax on whiskey distilled by small farmers in western Pennsylvania, who had no other way of selling surplus grain except by distilling. Jefferson warned that the tax was unwise because collecting it would commit "the authority of the government in parts where resistance is most probable."

But that was just what Alexander Hamilton, author of the tax, wanted. He was determined to give the new federal government an opportunity to demonstrate its strength and authority over the states. When the farmers resisted revenue agents who sought to enforce the tax, Hamilton helped raise and led 15,000 federal militia troops against them.

The farmers were routed violently. Eighteen of them were seized for trial in Philadelphia as traitors. Only two were convicted, however, and both were pardoned by President Washington when it became obvious that raising an army against a handful of desperate farmers had been a major political blunder.

The farmers' resistance had failed, but by provoking the government to overreact with a fierce display of power they alienated popular sympathy from the Federalist party and won votes for the Jeffersonians. Similarly, militants in modern resistance movements sometimes attempt to provoke police or troop brutality, in order to demonstrate graphically the inhumanity of the Establishment through the media's reports of such clashes.

The history of our nation is replete with examples of resistance movements that defied the law of the land in the spirit of Thoreau, who insisted, "I was not born to be forced." There has not been a single war fought by the

United States that has not been opposed by dissenters, many of whom went to jail rather than yield to the law.

Many other prominent resistance movements and events, admirable and otherwise, quickly come to mind— the Sons of Liberty, the Boston Tea Party, Shays' Rebellion, the newspaper editors' defiance of the Alien and Sedication Acts, New England's attempt to secede over Jefferson's election, the Burr plot to seize the government, the Nat Turner uprising, New York's anti-rent wars, John Brown's raids, the early communes, suffragette acts of resistance, the California vigilantes, the Know-Nothings, the Ku Klux Klan, the abolitionists, the Underground Railroad, the secession of the South, the Copperheads, anti-draft riots, Indian uprisings against Western expansion, the Molly Maguires, the I.W.W., the Haymarket affair, Carrie Nation's hatchet crusade, the Populists, Coxey's Army, the Pullman strike, the Ludlow Massacre, the speakeasies, Detroit's sit-down strikes, Christian Front riots, the civil rights movement, Birch Society crusades, Black Power, SDS (Students for a Democratic Society), the Weathermen, the Black Muslims and the White Citizens Council.*

Resistance movements may be good, bad or a mixture of both. But if there is one thing they definitely are not, obviously, it is un-American. Although most dissenters believe that nonviolence is the most persuasive way to resist, a minority feels that violence is "as American as apple pie."

"We are a rebellious nation," said abolitionist Theodore Parker. "Our whole history is treason: our blood was attainted before we were born; our creeds are infidelity to the mother church; our Constitution, treason to our fatherland. What of that? Though all the governors in the world bid us commit treason against man, and set an example, let us never submit."

Never before in our history have the worthiness of our society and its values been so agonizingly questioned as they are today. The young, especially, are challenging the justice and wisdom of a government which presumably reflects the opinions of a majority of its citizens.

Can the majority of Americans, indeed, be wrong? About Indochina? About amnesty for draft resisters? About censorship? About sterner punishment for law-breakers? About school bussing? About what constitutes an acceptable appearance? About what constitutes patriotism? About desirable life goals? About the treatment of the poor? About how schools ought to be run? About prayers in the school? About desirable television programs? About morality? About the life style of youth today? About an overwhelming choice for President?

Whether and when the majority is wrong or not, how far do dissenters have the right to go in resisting its will?

*For detailed accounts of these movements and events, see the author's books: *The Extremists, Treason In America: Disloyalty versus Dissent,* and *Hawks, Doves and the Eagle.*

3 How Far Should Resistance Go?

The American majority throughout history has traditionally been intolerant of intellectuals, distrusting their views as radical. As a consequence, points out British novelist D. H. Lawrence, Americans with the most enlightened opinions fear conflict with the majority, whose voice is the nation's will.

Not all resistance movements are liberal, of course, nor are all liberal movements necessarily right. It must be remembered, also, that conservative "backlash" movements like the anti-bussing resistance and the "Right-to-Life" anti-abortion resistance do serve to inhibit unbridled Government power and make it more responsive to individual rights. The Bill of Rights was not designed only for Americans who hold liberal views.

When the Supreme Court ruled in 1973 that state laws against abortion were unconstitutional, religious groups opposed to abortion denounced the decision and declared that they would continue to fight for anti-abortion legislation in one form or another.

They pointed out that the Supreme Court had been morally wrong in the Dred Scott decision of 1857, which held slaves to be property, and they reminded fellow citizens that those Americans who had resisted that decision were ultimately acknowledged to be right. Hence the justification for the hopes and determination of every impassioned minority whose views are repudiated by the government or by society at large.

The nature of any resistance movement is that it is automatically controversial, raising anew the question of minority rights under the law. The Bill of Rights, of course, protects the right of dissenters to protest publicly.

The First Amendment, designed to protect unpopular minorities against the majority, clearly states, "Congress shall make no law . . . abridging the freedom of speech or of the press; or of the right of the people peaceably to assemble and to petition the Government for a redress of grievances."

Without such a safeguard, most democracies would be as likely as dictatorships to forbid unpopular speech, minority religions and a dissenting press. Other amendments of the Bill of Rights protect minorities from being railroaded to prison, exile or the death chamber during times of public hysteria, no matter who is President or what party is in power.

These are the basic strengths of American democracy that prevent it from slipping into a totalitarian state.

But should a minority be free to *disobey*—not just to protest—any law it regards as unjust? If so, then why should anyone else obey laws he personally dislikes?

One argument against punishing a minority that defies the law is that it often proves more right eventually than the majority it opposes, as Eugene Debs contended. A modern instance is the Vietnam War, which the majority at first supported, only to agree later with the minority that it had been a tragic blunder.

Henrik Ibsen referred to his "fundamental principle in every field and domain: that the minority is always in the right." He used the character of Dr. Stockmann, in his famous play *Enemy of the People*, to explain his reasons:

"A fighter in the intellectual vanguard cannot possibly gather a majority around him. In ten years the majority will possibly occupy the standpoint which Dr. Stockmann held at the public meeting. But during those ten years the doctor will not have been standing still; he will still be at least ten years ahead of the majority. The majority, the mass, the mob, will never catch up with him; and he can never have the majority with him . . . . At the point where I stood when I wrote each of my books there now stands a tolerably compact crowd; but I myself am no longer there."

Ibsen was gloomy about the chances that an enlightened minority could bring about timely changes in any society. "There are actually moments," he wrote, "when the whole history of the world reminds one of a sinking ship; the only thing to do is to save oneself . . . . The masses, both at home and abroad, have absolutely no understanding of higher things."

But it is in the nature of the resister to be optimistic—to hope that by effectively resisting wrong laws and policies he can eventually persuade fellow citizens to change them. The question is often one of how long it takes. But reforms seldom come without the pressures built up by a dissatisfied minority. Tocqueville observed, "The citizens who form the minority associate in order, first to show their numerical strength and so to diminish the moral power of the majority."

Understandably, the majority challenges the assumption of the minority that it is right merely because it thinks or says that it is. Passionate convictions can always be found on both sides of controversial questions. The greater the heat, as a rule, the less the light. But where in disputes between majority and minority, is an acceptable judge to be found?

Locke wrote, "The people shall judge." But under the Constitution, the government is the voice of the people. And it is this voice—the voice of the majority—that the minority insists is wrong. The minority, which usually has studied a problem in great depth, considers the majority unqualified to judge it correctly.

In dealing with the American intervention in Vietnam, most people simply threw up their hands and said in effect, "It's all too complicated for us. We leave it to the President, who has all the information and knows best." But President and Congress alike are usually guided by a handful of alleged experts, as they were in making military interventions in the Bay of Pigs, the Dominican Republic and Indochina.

And the experts proved wrong in each case.

Although the resistance proved right in those instances, it is not always or automatically right, no matter how many of its adherents go to jail courageously as martyrs for their convictions. Nor is the majority morally right simply because the law is on its side, enabling it to tell those who protest, "You must do as we say because our numbers are greater than yours!"

Often neither majority nor minority has *absolute* right on its side. The complex bussing issue is an example. One side insists that without bussing black children to white schools, and white children to black schools, there can be no equality of American education. The other side insists that it is wrong to compel a child to be bussed miles away from his home, instead of letting him attend a neighborhood school, just for the sake of redressing racial imbalance in the schools.

Both are valid arguments. Justice might best be served in such cases not by the majority's forcing its will upon the minority, but by making the law flexible enough to take care of the just grievances of resisters. In social and moral questions, justice is often in the eye of the beholder.

Problems arise when the majority will neither listen nor compromise, even when its law violates Constitutional guarantees. The minority is often unwilling to suffer such a law for the years it may take before the Supreme Court reviews it.

"The right to defy an unconstitutional statute has its roots in our traditions of individualism and in our mistrust of the uncontrolled power of the state," observes Supreme

Court Justice William O. Douglas. That mistrust was written into numerous limitations on governmental power contained in the Constitution. The right to ignore a statute that is unconstitutional is a reflection of those limitations. Like them, it says: So far government may go and no further.

In pleading the cause of the South before the Civil War, Senator John C. Calhoun argued eloquently for the right of the governed to resist arbitrary acts by the government.

"No one can have a higher respect for the maxim that the majority ought to govern," he declared, "than I have . . . but where [people's interests] are dissimilar, so that the law that may benefit one portion may be ruinous to another, it would be, on the contrary, unjust and absurd to subject them to its will."

When the government does not respond to just grievances, Calhoun believed, the minority has a right and duty to nullify the controversial law where it can, leaving it up to the Supreme Court eventually to decide who is right.

Most governments of the world agree that there are higher laws than the law of any land. In the Nuremberg trials of German war criminals after World War II, we joined in the ruling that any citizen ordered to commit atrocities by his government, or any soldier by his army, has the duty to a "higher" law to refuse. Articles 90 to 92 of the Uniform Code of Military Justice of the U.S. Armed Forces now state that an American serviceman has an absolute right to disobey any unlawful order of a superior officer.

Citing these laws, Vietnam draft resisters refused to participate in what they considered an American crime of genocide being perpetrated against the people of Indochina. But the American government could not permit this civil disobedience without in effect admitting that its war was unlawful.

Almost all Americans agree that when Adolph Hitler ordered the mass murder of Jews, Poles and his political foes, Germans who resisted those orders were right and admirable, while those who obeyed were wrong and contemptible. But the American majority disputes the charge of the American resistance movement that the United States was guilty of the same genocide in Vietnam that the Nazis had practiced in Europe.

Presuming the right of a minority to resist laws it believes unjust, to what extent is it entitled to carry out this resistance? To the extent of simply refusing to cooperate with requirements of the law? Of destroying property in order to protest the law? Of blocking its enforcement physically? Of engaging in violence against its enforcers? Of destroying symbols like the American flag, or otherwise offending patriotic feelings, to express contempt for the government? Of advocating victory for the government's announced enemy?

Resistance, obviously, is a matter of degree. The government is faced with problems of different magnitude in coping with opposition to its policies by a student who expresses resistance by wearing an armband to school in mourning for the government's victims, and by a Weatherman who protests by blowing up banks, power stations or military projects.

Both the majority and minority of Americans were sickened by the escalating violence that marked the decade of the 1960s—the Chicago police riot at the Democratic Convention of 1968; Black Panther shoot-outs with police; violence on campuses; the assassinations of John F. Kennedy, Martin Luther King and Robert Kennedy; the seemingly endless bloody war in Indochina; the riots in the ghettos. All deplored violence directed against people, although they differed over the blame for it.

Some militants sought to dramatize their protest against the Vietnam War and neglect of the American poor by destroying property symbolic of the Establishment. Denounced for using violence, they replied that their victims were only objects made of paper, wood, stone or steel, whereas the government was employing bloody violence against people—in Vietnam, in the ghettos, on campus and in the streets. Resisters blamed the "silent majority" for tolerating and encouraging such violence.

Conservative spokesmen branded the dissenters as Communists, traitors and lawbreakers.

The resistance movement increasingly came to repudiate violence of any kind as a protest tactic, because it generally alienated more people than it shocked into reconsidering American policies. In turn, millions of Americans, sobered by the sordid fiasco of Vietnam, began to conclude that perhaps the resisters had been right about it and had actually been trying to save the country from a disastrous mistake.

Resistance generally begins as the alternative to violence in protesting injustice. The government and the majority that supports it have an important stake in listening thoughtfully to dissent. Only when dedicated citizens lose all hope of justice, as a rule, do they turn in despair to violent revolt.

A President or Congressman may justify ignoring a resistance movement by citing opinion polls—the voice of the majority. "If a poll back home shows me that fifty-five percent of my constituents favor the death penalty for insulting the American flag," one Congressman said dryly, "that's the way I'll vote—if I want to get reelected."

But a weathervane vote is not necessarily a just or moral vote. Americans' best interests are served by electing leaders, not followers, to office. Intelligent voting requires listening with an open mind to both sides of an issue—not just to the side that is largest or noisiest.

Those who resist the law must prove that they do so not lightly or selfishly but out of a genuine concern for justice. "Any tolerance that I might feel toward the disobeyer," declares Senator Philip A. Hart, "is dependent on his willingness to accept whatever punishment the law might impose."

Going to jail for one's beliefs, if necessary, is beyond question a testimony to one's sincerity. Some would question the justice of a society that requires this martyrdom, but it is certainly an almost universal practice.

"In Asia, Africa, and probably in South America . . . you haven't quite got your credentials unless you have a jail record," declared Scott Buchanan, late dean of St. John's college, Annapolis. "You are not quite decent. You're not certified as honest unless you have been to jail."

Many resisters themselves believe that they should be prepared to pay a penalty for breaking a law they consider unjust, simply because it *is* the law. But the real question would seem to be how severely they should be punished. Certainly justice would not seem to be served by keeping sincere war protesters behind bars for four years, while many embezzlers, armed robbers, dope peddlers, assaulters, arsonists and other criminals go free after one- to three-year prison terms.

Eugene Debs, who was sentenced to ten years in jail for publicly condemning World War I as an imperialist struggle for commercial markets, declared, "I have never advocated violence in any form. I have always believed in education, in intelligence, in enlightenment, and I have always made my appeal to the reason and conscience of the people . . . . When great changes occur in history, when great principles are involved, the majority are wrong. The minority are right!"

One wonders what principles of justice are served when the government deals with political prisoners on the same terms it accords to common criminals. Prison is presumably intended to rehabilitate the lawbreaker. Do we send the political resister to jail, then, to "rehabilitate" him out of his dissent and compel him to accept the majority view?

Many of those who join the resistance movement are pacifists or religious persons with a nonviolent philosophy, like that of Quakers and Catholic Workers. They believe that a just society cannot be achieved by using the violent methods of the unjust, and that each individual must purge himself of violent inclinations. Their view was shared in the Vietnam War by hippie demonstrators urging, "Make love, not war." Faced with the leveled rifles of troops called out to disperse them, they replied by placing flowers in the barrels of the guns.

Some who practice civil disobedience make a distinction between violence against persons and violence against property. They consider the latter a permissible tactic when it can help to save lives, directly or indirectly. A greater crime, as they see it, is to stand by passively without doing anything to resist injustice leveled against others.

Jo Ann Mulert was one of eight persons tried in Indianapolis for raids that destroyed draft board files and also Dow Chemical Company research files on nerve gas and napalm.

"I was brought up," she said, "according to Christian beliefs that said human lives are more important than property rights. I'm not sure what 'Christian' means, but I am sure that it doesn't mean keeping silent."

How far resistance can go is an elastic concept. There can be no one simple answer to cover the wide range of tactics. The government, representing the majority, disagrees with the minority as to what tactics of dissent are permissible.

Resisters may consider it a morally just act to destroy draft board files in order to save American boys from dying in an immoral war. But the law is on the side of the government, which simply ignores the moral issue and prosecutes the resisters under legal statutes that make no allowances for motive.

One group of thirty-five Columbia Law School professors defended the right of persons "whose voices might otherwise not be heard" to violate openly a law they disapprove of, if they are prepared to pay the penalty.

"Having in mind the difficulties sometimes experienced in drawing attention to public issues and to dissenting views," they declared, "we cannot condemn this form of civil disobedience in every conceivable instance."

The punishment of civil disobedience for principles is often a matter of selective justice. Sometimes the government decides not to prosecute resisters because there are too many of them in a controversial demonstration, and it may instead punish only a few leaders. Sometimes if a trial results in a hung jury, the prosecution will not retry the case, preferring to let it drop, particularly if sympathy has been created for the defendants as victims of political persecution.

At other times, if the government is determined to put the resisters behind bars, prosecution may be persistent and severe. Justice is never a very exact science. But it would be a mistake for resisters to be optimistic about the consequences of violating the letter of the law. In most cases the cost of defiance is a jail term or a stiff fine, or both.

Resistance movements all over the world have served mankind well in opposing the oppression of wilful governments against their own people and those of other countries.

Dissenters at home and abroad have proved that they are no less valuable to the course of true justice than the law itself. There can be no moral progress in any society without courageous individuals ready to go to jail in the struggle to awaken the conscience of their countrymen against injustice.

4 Four Giants Who Showed the Way

Nonviolent resistance movements often take their inspiration from one or more memorable figures in history whose example provides the courage and determination to endure all hardships suffered in the cause.

One of the earliest practitioners of the credo was the rebel Jesus Christ, as his story has come down to us in the history of the Bible. Jesus was the great teacher and exemplar of nonviolent resistance. He disagreed with the Pharisees that Jewish ritual must be observed above all else, including moral sincerity. The Pharisees attacked him for heresy—for preaching not God's word but his own.

His resistance won him the sympathy and support of the Judean masses. Acclaiming him their long-awaited Messiah, they sought to compel him to lead a political revolution against Roman rule. But he rejected the idea of seeking a better life on earth, urging instead pursuit of spirituality and communion with God. When many disappointed followers deserted him, he became a wandering missionary. His claim to be the son of God, reinforced by the miracles credited to him by the Bible, made him an awe-inspiring figure.

His growing cult alarmed the Pharisees, especially when he opposed wealth accumulated through business and finance. "You cannot serve God and money," Jesus warned, and he observed, "It is easier for a camel to go through a needle's eye than for a rich man to get into the kingdom of God."

His enemies sought to trap him into a dangerous defiance of Roman law by publicly asking him whether he agreed that taxes should be paid to Caesar. Jesus called attention to Caesar's picture on a Roman coin and replied, "Render to Caesar what belongs to Caesar, and to God what belongs to God."

In Jerusalem he led a demonstration against traders and money-changers who operated in the court of the Temple, driving them out for making God's house "a den of thieves." The priests, scribes and Pharisees he had denounced as unspiritual bureaucrats conspired to crush his resistance movement.

One of his disciples, Judas Iscariot, was bribed to betray him. His arrest was arranged in an olive grove outside the city to avoid provoking a riot. Brought before his Pharisee accusers, Jesus refused to renounce his claim to be the son of God and was branded guilty of blasphemy. The Roman procurator at Jerusalem, Pontius Pilate, ordered him executed as a rebel, and he was crucified with two thieves at Golgotha.

The legend of Christ was completed by reported miracles—that his body had vanished from the tomb, and that he had appeared after death to several disciples. His resurrection became the cornerstone of the Christian religion, giving believers hope of similarly rising from the dead to the Kingdom of Heaven.

Jesus became a world symbol of spiritual resistance to armed might. His refusal to lead a violent revolution against either the oppression of Rome or the Pharisee priests established the principle that noble ends do not justify violent means, which violate the spirit of brotherly love that Jesus taught.

The only violence Jesus advocated was driving the money-changers from the Temple, a symbolic act to demonstrate the cleansing of corrupt practices from religion. When Fathers Phil and Dan Berrigan burned draft files at Catonsville, N.J., they believed that they were engaged in a similar act of religious resistance and purification.

Another inspiring exemplar of nonviolent resistance was Henry Thoreau, who insisted on the right to lead his own life and resist the encroachment of government. In the summer of 1846, President James Polk took the country to war against Mexico on a pretext, in order to have an excuse for seizing what is now California, New Mexico and Texas.

Thoreau was living at the time an essentially hermit's existence, building a cabin on the shore of Walden Pond in Concord, Massachusetts, where he baked his own bread, raised garden vegetables, fished and trapped wild game. He sought to live as close as possible to nature, in communion with bird, beast and plant.

Like other abolitionists, Thoreau was convinced that the war with Mexico was an imperialist adventure to extend the area of slaveholding. He called it "the work of comparatively a few individuals using the standing government as their tool." Resisting the war the only way he knew how, he refused to pay a Massachusetts poll tax in protest. The town fathers of Concord imprisoned him behind two-foot-thick walls.

"As they could not reach me," he wrote, "they had resolved to punish my body . . . . I saw that the State was half-witted . . . . that it did not know its friends from its foes, and I lost all my remaining respect for it."

Hearing that his friend Thoreau had been jailed, Ralph Waldo Emerson hurried to the prison. "What are you doing in there, Henry?" he demanded in dismay.

"What are you doing out there, Waldo?" Thoreau replied.

Without Thoreau's knowledge and consent, his aunt hurriedly paid his tax, and he was released after a night in jail. Irked, he told the jailor, "I'll be back again next year. I will never pay tax to any government for an unjust cause."

In 1849 he wrote his famous tract *Civil Disobedience*, which echoed around the world for over a century. Sparking nonviolent resistance in one country after another, it strongly influenced Leo Tolstoi, Mahatma Gandhi, Norman Thomas and Martin Luther King.

Thoreau argued that legal processes of change are too slow to rectify injustice. "They take too much time," he wrote, "and a man's life will be gone . . . . If the injustice . . . is of such a nature that it requires you to be the agent of injustice to another, then, I say, break the law. Let your life be a counter-friction to stop the machine." This idea inspired the Students for a Democratic Society in the 1960s, leading to a decade of resistance attempts to "stop the machine."

In 1850, when Congress passed the Fugitive Slave Law to compel abolitionists to turn over runaway slaves to their masters in the South, Thoreau wrote, "My thoughts are murder to the State and involuntarily go to plotting against it." He became an active member of the Underground Railroad, helping fugitive slaves escape to Canada.

After John Brown and his followers had been arrested for the raid on Harper's Ferry to spark a slave uprising, Thoreau rang the bell in Concord's Town Hall. When citizens assembled, he told them, "I hear many condemn these men because they were so few. When were the good and the brave ever in the majority? . . . . Is it not possible that an individual may be right and a government wrong? Are laws to be enforced simply because they are made? Or declared by any number of men to be good, if they are not good?"

Thoreau warned his fellow Americans, "The law will

never make men free; it is men who have got to make the law free. They are the lovers of law and order who observe the law when the government breaks it."

As a young lawyer, English-trained Mohandas K. Gandhi went to South Africa to defend fellow Indians against discrimination by the Transvaal government. At first he dutifully upheld the law even though he himself was often treated as a "coolie," forcibly removed from first-class railway compartments and refused accommodation in hotels.

Reading Thoreau's essay on civil disobedience, Gandhi found it "so convincing and truthful" that he became a lifelong disciple, always carrying a copy of the essay to jail with him. He told Roger Baldwin of the American Civil Liberties Union (ACLU) that it contained the essence of his political philosophy. Gandhi held that the individual was morally superior to the state because he was a person, while the state was nothing but a bloodless corporate structure.

Calling his adaptation of Thoreau's nonviolent civil disobedience *satyagraha* ("firmness in truth"), Gandhi led the struggle of Indians against South African oppression for twenty years. To steel himself for the hardships of a life of poverty and jail, he lived as simply as possible, subsisting on an austere diet of wholemeal bread, peanut butter, fruit and goat's milk. In and out of prison most of his life, he often went on hunger strikes to dramatize his cause.

Yet he was careful not to call himself a revolutionary. His aim was not to overthrow the government but to make it just. He warned his followers that to justify their resistance to unjust laws, they must first show themselves generally obedient to the laws of the state, and in that way remain bona fide members of the whole society.

Thousands of dedicated resisters mobilized by his South African satyagraha were punished by forced labor in the mines. Some were flogged and shot. Gandhi went to jail for a year. But his civil disobedience campaign aroused so much sympathy throughout the British Empire that the South African government felt compelled to rescind some of its harsher policies.

Gandhi returned to India in 1914. Giving away all his possessions, he took to wearing a loin cloth to symbolize his bonds with the poor who could afford no other clothing. Millions joined his satyagraha against the British rule that kept India in economic and political subjugation, and also against the caste system that made outcasts of Untouchables.

Leading open resistance to unjust laws, he urged his followers to submit peacefully to penalties: "The law-breaker breaks the law surreptitiously and tries to avoid the penalty; not so the civil resister . . . when he considers certain laws to be so unjust as to render obedience to them a dishonor. He then openly and civilly breaks them and quietly suffers the penalty of the breach . . . . Freedom must be sought behind prison walls."

Gandhi demanded strict self-discipline from his followers, particularly passive resistance when attacked. Often they were beaten, clubbed, trampled upon and kicked. But they remained limp under all blows. When a first rank was beaten down, police or troops then had to attack a second, a third, and a fourth rank. In the end the Indians won by sheer force of numbers and persistence in martyrdom.

On occasion a conscience-stricken judge would tell the bony little ascetic leader, "Oh, we won't send you to jail now."

Gandhi would reply simply, "It's your duty, Mr. Justice, to send me to jail."

Inspired Indians willingly gave up their lives for him. When a fifteen-year-old boy was sentenced to be flogged, at each stroke of the whip until he lost consciousness he cried out fervently, "Long live Gandhi!"

Gandhi urged his followers to return love for hatred, to renounce violence, to eat and drink sparingly, to give away all possessions, and to cherish their own cultural heritage. To compel England to yield to Indian demands, he led a boycott on British-made cloth. The spinningwheel became his symbol of resistance as Indians spun their own cloth.

In 1930 he called for resistance to the unpopular Salt Act. The British monopoly on salt manufacturing in India became a symbol in the struggle for independence, exactly like the tea tax fought by American colonists in 1773. Gandhi led a Salt March to the coast to defy the law publicly by collecting salt from the sea where it had evaporated on mudflats.

Government forces attacked and jailed sixty thousand of the Salt Marchers, even machine-gunning a crowd and killing seventy people. But so strong was Gandhi's influence that not a hand was raised against the rain of blows from police clubs. "My ambition is no less than to convert the British people through nonviolence," he declared, "and thus make them see the wrong they have done to India."

By August 1947 he succeeded. The British, dedicated to the principles of justice, compelled their government to yield to Gandhi's resistance and grant India independence.

Both Thoreau and Gandhi inspired Martin Luther King in his struggle for civil rights in America. When Mrs. Rosa Parks was arrested in Alabama for refusing to sit in the back of the bus, Thoreau's essay on civil disobedience gave King an idea for black resistance. He organized a boycott of Montgomery's segregated busses to enforce their integration.

"We were simply saying to the white community," he wrote, " 'We can no longer tend our cooperation to an evil system.' . . . . From this moment on I conceived of our

movement as an act of massive noncooperation." He kept
the boycott going until a court ruling ended segregated
seating.

Like Gandhi, King sought to change the hearts of whites,
to move them toward social justice. In imitation of the Salt
March, he led march after march of demonstrators to
protest the denial of civil rights to blacks.

In 1963, Birmingham police used police dogs and fire
hoses against King's peaceful demonstrators, creating nationwide indignation and sympathy for the black cause.
Jailed for five days, King urged his followers to remain
nonviolent, declaring, "We must not lose faith in our
white brothers." He encouraged them with the confident
and prayerful anthem of the civil rights movement, "We
Shall Overcome."

To resist voter discrimination against blacks, in April
1965 he led a dramatic fifty-four-mile march of thirty thousand blacks and whites from all over the country, from
Selma to Montgomery. When police tried to break up the
march with tear gas, clubs and whips, King told the
demonstrators, "If cursed, do not curse back. If pushed, do
not push back. If struck do not strike back, but evidence
love and goodwill at all times."

Television cameramen recorded the police attack, out-
raging public opinion and winning new supporters for
King's movement.

To demand open housing, he led peaceful marches
through rock-throwing mobs in Chicago's white neigh-
borhoods in 1966. In 1967 he led demonstrations to end the
Vietnam War and devote American energies to reform at
home. He went to Memphis in March, 1968, to help black
sanitation workers there demand a living wage. Ad-
dressing a crowd, he revealed that threats were constantly
being made against his life.

"But it doesn't really matter with me now," he said, "because I've been to the mountaintop . . . . And I've looked
over, and I've seen the promised land." Three days later,
like Mahatma Gandhi, he was assassinated.

President Lyndon B. Johnson ordered a national day of mourning, pleading with civil rights leaders to keep furious blacks of America from rioting. "No one could doubt what Martin Luther King would want," he appealed. "That his death should be the cause of more violence would deny everything he worked for." But no one could cool black wrath.

Without King's restraining hand, racial rioting exploded in twenty-nine states, marked by arson (2,600 fires), looting, destruction, attacks on policemen and firemen, and gun battles in the street. It was a grim reminder to Americans that the way of nonviolent resistance—the way of Jesus, Thoreau, Gandhi and King—was to be cherished and encouraged.

"If justice is to be achieved," declared former Attorney General Ramsey Clark, "there will be times when conscience may compel an individual to say, This is wrong and I will not obey. Thoreau, Gandhi, and Martin Luther King did. They affected history by doing so and enriched justice."

5 Resisting the Hitler Terror

Nonviolent resistance must be tolerated to a point under a constitutional democracy, but under a dictatorship it is quickly and ruthlessly suppressed. Dissenters often have no practical choice but submission or revolutionary violence.

When Adolf Hitler took power in Germany in 1933, he was opposed by Pastor Dietrich Bonhoeffer, who regarded him as the Antichrist and believed it a Christian duty to "eliminate him." Bonhoeffer joined a group of high-ranking conspirators who intended to kill Hitler and restore the German republic. When the conspiracy was exposed, he was arrested and executed. Three other members of his family also died in the Resistance.

Another German pastor, Martin Niemoller, originally welcomed the Nazis to power, inspired by their pledge to revive a proud German nationalism. Disillusioned by Hitler's paganism, anti-Semitism and tyranny, he organized a public protest. Threatened with arrest, he defied the Nazis from his pulpit.

"We have no more thought of using our powers to escape the arm of the authorities than had the Apostles of old," he declared. "No more are we ready to keep silent at man's behest when God commands us to speak . . . . We must obey God rather than man." Arrested four days later as an enemy of the state, he spent eight years in a concentration camp until liberated by victorious Allied troops.

"Under Hitler, opposition to government was equated with treason," observed historian Henry Steele Commager. "Those who dared question the inferiority of Jews, or the justice of the conquest of inferior peoples like the Poles, were effectually silenced, by exile or by the gas chamber. With criticism and dissent eliminated, Hitler and his followers were able to lead their nation, and the world, down the path to destruction."

Hitler's mad war policies brought some high-ranking officers in the German Army and Nazi bureaucracy into the Resistance. German editor Paul Scheffer explained why they did not resign their commissions or posts: "The state is so overpowering that one is compelled to play according to its rules, even if one is out to destroy it."

When Admiral Wilhelm Canaris, chief of the Abwehr, Nazi military counterintelligence, visited the smoking ruins of Warsaw, he was shaken and nauseated by the spectacle of human suffering caused by Nazi brutality. He burst into tears, confiding to his adjutant, "I simply can't go on."

Joining the Resistance, he used his authority to provide a smokescreen for the activities of young officers who were sabotaging the Nazi party and the Gestapo. Playing a double game, Canaris pretended ardent loyalty to the Fuehrer while subtly sabotaging his orders in clever ways. He even managed to smuggle hunted Jews out of the country as Abwehr "agents."

The information network of the Abwehr was put at the disposal of the Resistance, so that its members always knew to what extent they were suspected by the Gestapo. After participating in an unsuccessful attempt on Hitler's life, Canaris was exposed, arrested, and hanged from a meathook.

Major General Hans Oster sought to break Hitler's spell over the German people by plotting to have him seized and declared insane. When the plot failed, Oster sent warnings to the Dutch and Scandinavians about Hitler's plans to attack them. Arrested for trying to get Pastor Bonhoeffer released from prison, he was hanged for treason.

The Resistance plot which came closest to succeeding was that of high-ranking officers to assassinate Hitler in July 1944. After several abortive attempts, Colonel Graf von Stauffenberg managed to smuggle a time bomb concealed in a briefcase into a conference at Hitler's field headquarters. The explosion failed to kill Hitler but pierced his eardrums, paralyzed his right arm and burned his leg. Stauffenberg and his fellow conspirators were shot in a courtyard.

Perhaps the most famous military member of the German Resistance was Field-Marshal Erwin Rommel, commander of the largest Nazi army in the West. He secretly plotted to have Hitler arrested and tried by a German court while a new German government sought surrender terms from the Allies. Arrested and charged with high treason, he was allowed to commit suicide.

A resistance group called the Kreisau Circle was led by Count Helmuth von Moltke, who wrote to an English friend, "The constant danger in which we live is formidable. . . . Can you imagine what it means to work as a group when you cannot use the telephone, when you are unable to post letters, when you cannot tell the names of your closest friends to your other friends for fear that one might be caught and might divulge the names under the pressure?"

He was arrested and executed when one of his circle exposed him under torture by the Gestapo. Facing his executioners, he said defiantly, "Make us into a legend!"

Germany also had a Youth Resistance made up of Left-wing students and followers of Bishop Galen of Munster, who urged, "It may be that obedience to God and loyalty to conscience will cost you or me our lives, our freedom,

or our home. But let us rather die than sin." Joining the
Hitler Youth as a blind, young resisters distributed underground messages and leaflets and helped men hunted by
the Gestapo to escape.

The group known as the White Rose began in Munich in
1942 when a medical student asked his friends, "Isn't it
preposterous that we sit in our rooms and study how to
heal mankind, when on the outside the state every day
sends countless young people to their death? What in the
world are we waiting for? Until one day the war is over
and all nations point to us and say that we accepted this
government without resisting?"

Acquiring a duplicating machine, they put out a series of
anti-Nazi leaflets, mailing thousands to people chosen
from the phone books of various cities. "It is certain that
today every honest German is ashamed of his
government," one leaflet declared. " . . . . Offer passive
resistance—*resistance*—wherever you may be, forestall
the spread of this atheistic war machine before it is too
late . . . . . Do not forget that every people deserves the
regime it is willing to endure."

They called for sabotage of every phase of the war effort. Risking their own lives at night, they painted "Down
With Hitler" in black tar on house walls, university columns, theatres and government buildings.
Many were caught and executed.

When the Nazi armies overran France in 1940, most
French hesitated between collaboration for survival, and
resistance at the risk of prison, torture or death. The most
courageous joined the Free French underground, which
spread defiance through its illegal newspaper, *Le
Résistance.*

At its height, the French Resistance claimed a great
secret army of over 300,000. At first it fought the Nazi occupation as guerrillas, while disparaging Charles de
Gaulle's Free French movement. But in the spring of 1943
the French Communist party took over leadership of the
Resistance.

the French Communist party took over leadership of the
Resistance, the Nazis ordered fifty to a hundred hos-

When the Nazis banned all books extolling French culture and the ideals of the French Revolution, author Jean
Bruller set up a secret publishing house called the Mid-
night Press. Under the pseudonym Vercours he printed
forbidden books that were smuggled past the Gestapo by
dignified ladies in bulging shopping bags on thei
bicycles, or in armfuls of packages they clutched on the
French Metro. Vercours' books helped encourage French
resistance to Nazi propaganda.

The concentration camps began to fill with French
peasants and workers who refused to inform on the
Resistance, youths who scrawled the Cross of Lorraine on
walls, and schoolteachers who led their pupils in singing
the *Marseillaise*. Some prisoners courageously sacrificed
their lives to encourage resistance in the camps. In his
Anti-Memoirs, Andre Malraux describes the courage of
one woman prisoner:

"The female commandant rides her bicycle alongside a
column of prisoners on their way to work. She gets off,
walks up to a prisoner and slaps her face, perhaps for
being out of line. The latter, leader of a Resistance network and aware of the consequences of what she is about
to do, slaps the SS woman back with all her strength. The
whole column gasps. SS men and women lash out wildly
with their whips. They set the dogs on the prisoner, but
her blood is trickling over her feet, and instead of biting
her the dogs lick it up, as in the Christian legends. The SS,
not so sentimental, drive the dogs away and beat her to
death. The tears flow silently down the cheeks of the
prisoners standing there at attention."

Just before D-Day, under direct orders from Allied
headquarters, the Resistance cut transportation and communication lines, and engaged German forces in battle.
"The acts of sabotage multiplied," reported Vercours,
"the Resistance everywhere was blowing up bridges, factories, transformers. In three weeks *Résistance-Fer* [the

Railway Resistance] alone destroyed more locomotives than Allied bombs in three months."

In his own village, the Nazis compelled Vercours and his neighbors to guard high-tension pylons at night. By arrangement with the R istance, men on watch brought along rope which the saboteurs used to tie them up, after which the pylons were blown up.

In an effort to stop attacks on German forces by the Resistance, the Nazis ordered fifty to a hundred hostages rounded up and shot for every German killed. At Oradour-sur-Glane they shot every able-bodied man in the village, burned down every house, then filled a church with women, children and old people and set fire to it. Almost thirty thousand French hostages were executed, and another forty thousand were killed in French prisons.

In the occupied Netherlands, schoolboys did what they could to resist their Nazi conquerors. When the Germans forbade the showing of the Dutch flag, students spread word of a resistance campaign to have everyone wear white carnations, favorite flower of the Prince of the Netherlands. Angry Nazis began yanking them out of buttonholes. Dutch youth then spread the word to break up small pieces of old razor blades and hide them among the flower petals.

On dark nights youth groups put up false road signs that sent Nazi vehicles plunging into the canals. They also cut telephone wires at night. One morning the Nazis awoke to find half of Amsterdam's telephone system put out of order.

But perhaps in no other country was the Resistance so universal and determined as in Denmark. As soon as the Nazis set foot in that little nation, copies of Thoreau's *Civil Disobedience* flooded the country. Even King Christian took part in acts of mass civil disobedience that enraged the Nazis.

The Danes had a long tradition of democratic attitudes and institutions, with a stubborn insistence on freedom of speech and press; they had suffered damage to these institutions from earlier German invasions. Dedicated to a cooperative society based on the conviction that each citizen is stronger for cooperating with fellow Danes, the country's patriots joined hands firmly against the Nazis.

Four hours after the first Germans entered Copenhagen, seventeen-year-old Arne Sejr and his school friends distributed copies of a leaflet, *Ten Commandments for Danes*. It read in part: "1. You must not go to work in Germany or Norway. 2. You must work badly for the Germans . . . . 4. You must spoil their production machines and tools . . . . 6. You must delay all German transports . . . 8. You must not buy or trade with the Nazis . . . . 10. You must defend every person persecuted by the Germans. JOIN THE FIGHT FOR DENMARK'S FREEDOM!"

The Danish government resigned, going underground as the Freedom Council. Danish laborers dumped pounds of sugar into the cement they mixed for German gun emplacements so that the mounts crumpled the first time the guns were fired. Copenhagen postmen tore up letters to the Gestapo from suspected informers. Furniture vans and beer trucks delivered concealed explosives and weapons to Resistance groups.

Defying Nazi censorship, the Resistance press of Denmark published six hundred underground newspapers during the war, circulating a total of twenty-six million copies. One Resistance paper was even printed in Braille for the blind.

When the Nazis sought to round up Danish Jews for concentration camps, the Resistance rallied the whole nation to save its Jewish population. Before the Gestapo could spread its dragnet, Danish Jews were snatched to safety by neighbors and taxi drivers. They were hidden in hospitals, attics, cellars, churches and institutions. Children stood guard against surprise raids until they

could be spirited away to neutral Sweden concealed in
Danish custom boats, harbor patrol launches, police boats,
freighters and fishing trawlers.

Out of 8,000 Danish Jews, the Danes helped no less than
7,200 to escape under the noses of the baffled Nazis.

On Midsummer Night, 1944, an occasion which the
Danes celebrate much as Americans celebrate the Fourth
of July, the German blackout was violated by an outbreak
of fireworks and skyrockets from Copenhagen's beloved
Tivoli amusement park. The public address system in the
Town Hall tower played *Tipperary* and other Allied songs
as crowds in the enormous Town Hall Square cheered and
laughed. Leaflets flooded through the crowds hailing the
defiant spirit of "fighting Denmark."

Infuriated, the Nazis dynamited the Tivoli and imposed
an 8:00 P. M. curfew. It was promptly violated by hundreds
of thousands of Danes who took evening strolls around
Copenhagen's suburbs. When several hundred were arrested, sixty dryly claimed innocence by virtue of having
been "sleepwalking."

To enforce the curfew, German patrols began riding
through evening crowds firing light machine guns. The
Danes tore up paving-stones to build street barricades top-
ped by the Danish flag, and set huge bonfires in which
they burned oil-soaked swastikas and pictures of Hitler.
The Resistance called a general strike. Every shop, factory
and office in Copenhagen shut down.

The Nazis declared martial law. Nazi Administrator
Werner Best swore to bring the Danes to their knees or ex-
terminate them all. He ringed Copenhagen with Panzer
divisions as thousands in the Resistance began escaping
through the city's sewers. Ordered to round them up, the
whole Danish police force refused and was sent to
concentration camps.

The Freedom Council refused to call off the general
strike until the Nazis had agreed to order its hated
Schalburg Corps out of the city, stop shooting innocent
people, and end the curfew. The Danish Resistance radio

continued broadcasting in the underground, the only clandestine network operated entirely from within a Nazi-oc-
cupied country. It arranged for trawlers plying between
Denmark and Sweden to bring in supplies of British
propaganda and war materials for the Resistance.

Danish saboteurs gave the Germans no rest. Three
Danish frogmen set explosives on four German warships
in Copenhagen harbor and blew them to pieces. Other
saboteurs specialized in blowing up German troop trains.
General Bernard Montgomery credited them with having
stopped every Danish train for two crucial weeks during
the Battle of the Bulge, preventing the Germans from getting reinforcements to the front.

The Danes also drove the Germans frantic by coor-
dinated slowdowns in factories producing vital war materials. "The Germans could find no effective way of
dealing with it," noted British military expert Basil Liddel
Hart. "At intervals, exasperated, they insisted on the removal of some particular administrator whom they
suspected of such practices—but he bequeathed his policy
and plans to his successor."

The Nazis tried desperately to smash the Resistance by
torturing captured suspects. Ruth Philipsen of the
Freedom Council knew the whereabouts and activities of
every member. Captured, she kept silent even when the
Gestapo beat her, yanked her hair, put thumb screws on
her fingers and threatened to kill her. Most who refused to
talk were shot.

Perhaps nothing damaged German morale more than
the Danish use of laughter as a weapon. The Nazis could
shrug off hate but could not endure ridicule. According to
Victor Borge, the Danes began to knit and wear little
woollen "beanie" caps with the British Royal Air Force
red, white and blue rosette insignia. The Nazis were
forced to issue an absurd order forbidding the wearing of
red, white and blue beanies.

In a bookstore displaying English books, the sign read:
"Think of the future—learn English." When the Nazis

ordered the English books replaced by German volumes, the proprietor complied with a new sign: "Learn German—while there is still time." The angry Nazis then insisted that the window display glorify the Rome-Berlin Axis. So between pictures of Hitler and Mussolini, the proprietor placed a single book by a famous Frenchman: *Les Miserables.*

On a newspaper kiosk Nazis were enraged to find that one Dane had scrawled: TO HELL WITH HITLER, but even more infuriated by a second scrawl beneath it: SORRY, I DON'T WANT HIM (SIGNED) THE DEVIL. On a circular shoulder-high brick street barrier in which Nazi MPs stood for protection, someone posted a mocking sign: THIS NAZI IS WEARING NO PANTS.

The Danes also made it personally clear to the Nazis that they were despised. Danish girls refused to date them. People refused to smile or nod at them. Typical of the spirit of the Resistance was a phone call that came one morning to Gestapo headquarters complaining about a swastika flying over an official building and demanding its removal.

"Unfortunately, that is impossible," replied a Nazi.

"In that case a Danish soldier will be sent to remove it."

"He will be shot if he tries."

"I am the soldier," said the caller. "You are speaking to the King of Denmark." The swastika was lowered.

On Hitler's express orders, Resistance attacks on Nazi forces were avenged "on the proportion of five to one." Of four million Danes, thirty-thousand were active members of organized Resistance groups. Three thousand were killed, apart from other Danes shot in reprisal for Resistance activities.

In occupied Norway, twelve thousand of the country's fourteen thousand teachers refused to join a Nazi Teachers' Front or force their classes to enroll in a Nazi Youth movement. When arrests were made all over the country, crowds followed the teachers to the railroad station, shouting encouragement and defying SS threats to open fire. The teachers were herded into unheated cattle cars, taken to a concentration camp and tortured.

Members of the Norwegian Resistance burned down the Oslo Central Labor Exchange, destroying all card indexes the Nazis used for forced labor. Others gathered and sent intelligence to England that enabled British bombers to wreck a new U-boat base in Trondheim Harbor. Youth in the Resistance helped British commandos dropped by parachute to carry out dangerous and important sabotage missions.

The Resistance was also operative in occupied Poland.

"Hucksters are capable of rising to heroic deeds," reported Maria Brzeska in 1944, "such as the time they fought to release truckloads of children who were being carried off to Germany. The small urchins selling cigarettes and matches are also skilled at selling secret, illegal papers and periodicals . . . .

"Numbers of peasants and workers have joined the ranks of the underground with a fervent desire to fight . . . for a Poland of free people. The vigorous development of the peasant press at a time when every printed page may have to be paid for with a human life is the finest proof of this spiritual and intellectual uplift of the village."

In April, 1943, when Heinrich Himmler ordered SS General Juergen Stroop to take sixty thousand Warsaw Jews to extermination camps, the Polish Resistance smuggled in a few pistols, rifles, homemade grenades and machine guns to the ghetto. As Stroop invaded the ghetto with tanks, artillery, flamethrowers and dynamite squads, the Jews fought back from vaults, cellars and sewers. The shocked Germans, who had expected no resistance, were forced to withdraw.

Renewing the attack later, Stroop wrote irritably, "The Jews and criminals resisted from base to base and escaped at the last moment." He could not understand why "this trash and subhumanity" did not give up and submit to liquidation. After several days he was forced to report fresh difficulty: "Over and over again new battle groups consisting of twenty to thirty Jewish men, accompanied by a corresponding number of women, kindled new resistance." He complained that the women were "firing pistols with both hands," and hurling grenades that they carried in their underclothes.

Setting fire to the ghetto, Stroop sought to burn the Jewish Resistance out. But most of the defenders preferred to continue resisting until they perished in the flames. Over seven thousand died in the hopeless struggle, but to Hitler's rage they fought off the Nazis for a whole month and killed several hundred before they perished.

The Czechs also mounted a fierce resistance against their Nazi conquerors. Priests of the Karl Borromaeus Church in Prague concealed 120 members of the Czech underground, two of whom assassinated Reinhard Heydrich, deputy chief of the Gestapo and boss of the Czech occupation.

In revenge, ten truckloads of SS troops surrounded the village of Lidice, chosen as a scapegoat, and wiped it off the face of the earth. Almost two hundred men, women and children were murdered, and 195 women were taken to concentration camps. Then the village was burned down and its ruins were dynamited.

Throughout Europe members of the Resistance put their lives on the line every day to resist the Nazi juggernaut by shooting German guards; blowing up Nazi trains, ships and installations; killing informers and Quislings.

But there were also nonviolent members of the Resistance who risked their lives by gathering intelligence for the Allies, by printing and distributing underground newspapers and leaflets, by helping shot-down Allied pilots escape, by hiding Jewish refugees, by cutting communications, by running Nazi blockades, by organizing strikes and slowdowns, and by exposing the Nazis to ridicule.

Perhaps the Resistance alone would not have been enough to end the nightmare years of the Nazi terror. But it was an invaluable auxiliary to the Allies, disorganizing Hitler's forces and keeping them off balance. By weakening the Nazis' ability to fight off the Allied invasion of the continent, and by uniting the people against Fascism, the Resistance shortened the time needed to restore freedom to Europe.

6 Resistance Movements Around the World

Since World War II there have been at least thirty prominent resistance movements around the world, about half of them undeclared wars of national liberation. The liberation of countries from Axis tyranny inspired a desire among people everywhere to be rid of dictators and colonial rulers.

Well-organized resistance movements that had fought Fascism in the underground sought to establish liberal or left-wing governments. But they were often thwarted by Allied occupation forces, which restored to power conservative Old Guard governments that had ruled before the war. As a consequence civil war broke out in Greece, Algeria and Vietnam.

Resistance to colonialism grew steadily with a postwar increase in the number of young people the colonial powers sent to institutions of higher learning. University education opened their eyes to the shortcomings of their societies and the need for change. When they returned home, instead of becoming instruments of the colonial powers, they aroused their people to join resistance movements and demand independence.

Normally placid Canada found itself with a major resistance movement on its hands when six million

French Canadians, long dissatisfied with their treatment as a minority by sixteen million English-speaking Canadians, threatened the secession of Quebec. Denouncing Protestant arrogance and intolerance toward Catholics, they complained of the same kind of second-class citizenship that blacks suffered in white America.

Their resistance galvanized the Canadian government into making reforms that gave university advantages to more French Canadians and opened up more executive positions in Quebec to them as graduates. But these reforms changed little for the French Canadian masses. Young workers joined the Quebec Liberation Front (FLQ). Although the FLQ was pledged to nonviolent resistance, one militant faction went underground, bombed 250 targets and kidnapped officials as hostages.

Their terror tactics not only failed to achieve FLQ objectives but also alienated English-speaking Canadians who blamed all separatists for the violence of a handful.

During the Cold War era the United States assumed the role of "world policeman," seeking to suppress both resistance and revolutionary movements around the world that it considered sympathetic to either the Soviet Union or Communist China.

In September, 1963, a military coup in the Dominican Republic overthrew elected President Juan Bosch, who had undertaken a program of social reform disliked by American big business interests. Two years later Bosch's supporters sought to restore him to office. Seizing strategic sections of the capital, they fought off attacks by the military junta.

President Lyndon B. Johnson sent 21,000 American troops to the island to "protect American lives." But TV news cameramen filmed them helping the junta against the Resistance, which was not strong enough to withstand the intervention.

Senator William Fulbright consistently opposed American involvement in civil wars that were inevitable where "feudal oligarchies resist all meaningful change by peaceful means." He declared, "In the case of the Dominican Republic, we did close our minds to the causes and to the essential legitimacy of revolution in a country in which democratic procedures had failed."

In Chile a resistance movement grew in the 1960s against big landowners who kept 200,000 rural families landless, and against over a hundred American corporations that took profit margins of thirty-five percent and higher out of the country while masses of Chilean workers lived in abject poverty.

Keeping the movement nonviolent, the Resistance elected Marxist Salvador Allende President in 1970, despite an attempt by the American International Telephone and Telegraph corporation to spend a million dollars in bribes to buy the election for his opponents.

Allende nationalized copper mines owned by three U.S. companies, raised workers' wages and gave peasants land. The loss of American economic aid caused severe problems for Chile but failed to swerve Allende from carrying out his pledges to the Resistance. The Chile experiment of Socialism by ballot, ended by a military coup and Allende's suicide in September, 1973, was a test case for the possibility of peaceful change by the resistance movements of Latin America.

In northern Ireland, Catholic resistance to Protestant English rule broke out once more in 1968. As a one-third minority in Ulster, the Catholics suffered from the poorest housing, the lowest-paying jobs, the greatest unemployment, the poorest schools, and the largest number of arrests, jailings and adverse court decisions.

Nonviolent civil rights marches began in August, led by 21-year-old Bernadette Devlin, fiery member of the British Parliament from the Ulster ghettos. Police beat demonstrators down with clubs. When they attacked a second march, Devlin shouted through a megaphone, "Everybody sit down as quickly as possible and then we'll see who's causing the violence!" The sudden mass sit-down caused the Ulster police to fall all over the demonstrators as TV newsmen filmed proof that the lawmen, not the Resistance, were creating the disorders.

The civil rights movement, noted Conor Cruise O'Brien, Irish Labor Party deputy in the Eire parliament, "encouraged the Catholics, and helped them to win important and long-overdue reforms." But militants impatient with the slow pace of change joined an underground Irish Republican Army (IRA). Bombings, shooting and arson brought counterviolence from militant Protestants, resulting in fierce street battles.

As northern Ireland fell into civil war, England rushed troops to Belfast and Londonderry to try to restore peace. Their presence only infuriated both sides, leading to new levels of terror, with rioting, bombings, arson and wanton murder daily occurrences. The British made sweeping arrests of IRA suspects and kept them in detention. Catholic men, women and children were killed in street battles. In reprisal, IRA rebels shot British troops, and in March, 1973, blew up areas of London with almost two hundred civilian casualties.

The world was appalled by the tragic spectacle of wholesale bloodshed that had stemmed from the failure of the Ulster government to deal realistically and fairly with the Resistance at the outset. "When will armies and police and government learn that violence begets only violence," asked New York political leader Herman Badillo, "that the use of arms is more often the catalyst of violence than a deterrent, that an army of occupation serves only to stiffen the resolve of the citizenry?"

In Algeria, between 1954 and 1962, growing nationalism led to a strong resistance movement against French rule. When the French refused to heed Algerian grievances, the Resistance organized the revolutionary *Front National de Liberation.*

French troops and police unleashed a campaign of brutal terror against the FLN. Algerian men, women and children suspected of collaboration were tortured for information, in France as well as in Algeria. When a book called *The Gangrene* exposed these tortures, French police suppressed it.

One victim testified in the book, "I have learned that since my arrest my three uncles have been shot. My torture is nothing compared with that of my brothers and sisters in Algeria—burned alive, mutilated, humiliated, violated, impaled and cut to pieces . . . . The only reason I give this evidence is that I hope my voice . . . will have a better chance of being heard." It was heard.

French intellectuals angrily aroused the French people. "When the government of a country allows crimes to be committed in its name," wrote Simone de Beauvoir, "every citizen thereby becomes a member of a collectively criminal nation."

Albert Camus said in anguish, "I should like to be able to love my country and still love justice."

A large and influential French resistance compelled Charles de Gaulle to stop the tortures and negotiate with the FLN, which finally won Algerian independence in July, 1962.

In neighboring Tunisia, resistance to French rule had been carried on by Habib Bourguiba, founder of the underground Neo-Destour (New Constitution) party. For twenty years he was a marked man, spending most of his time in prison, in exile or hiding from the French. Tunisians hid him, slipped food to him in prison, and carried out his secret orders sent from jail or exile. The persistence of the Tunisian resistance bore fruit in 1956, when French Prime Minister Pierre Mendes-France agreed to yield independence to the Tunisians.

Hitler's massacre of six million Jews during World War II won world sympathy for the Zionist movement that demanded a Jewish homeland where Jews would be safe from persecution.

Zionist leaders Chaim Weizmann and Ben Gurion led an immigration movement to British-governed Palestine. When Arab nationalists attacked the settlers, Britain restricted Jewish immigration to a limit of 75,000. Gurion and Weizmann led a resistance movement that brought Jewish refugees into Palestine past the British naval blockade.

A group called the Irgun defended Jewish settlements against Arab attacks. Some of the Irgun, known as the Stern Gang, used terror tactics against both the British and the Arabs but were disavowed by the nonviolent Resistance.

Zionist resistance eventually forced Britain to turn the country over to the United Nations. In November, 1947, the United Nations decreed that Britain must leave Palestine by August 1948, after which the country would be divided into one Arab and one Jewish state. But violent fighting broke out between Arabs and Zionists. The British frequently aided the Arabs for political reasons. The Irgun joined the Stern Gang in replying to terror tactics with counterterror.

The Arab states refused to recognize the new state of Israel. A resistance movement sprang up among the seventy thousand Palestinian Arabs who had been displaced by the Jewish state. Israel ignored them, insisting that the refugees were an Arab, not an Israeli, problem. Palestinian guerrillas who raided Israeli outposts were killed or imprisoned.

A terrorist band of Palestinians known as the Black September gang vowed to compel freedom for all Arab political prisoners in Israel and to overthrow the Jewish state. They led worldwide guerrilla raids on Israeli airliners, on Israeli athletes at the Olympics in Germany, and on Israeli embassies. They mailed letter bombs to Israeli diplomats abroad.

Blaming the United States for its support of Israel, they kidnapped two American officials in the Sudan, and murdered them when Israel refused to release its Arab political prisoners. The Israelis struck back with air raids and commando attacks on Palestinian guerrilla camps in Lebanon. They also shot down a Libyan airliner with a loss of 106 lives.

"The most deplorable aspect of the whole affair," observed *The Nation* in March 1973, "is that the Palestinians have a genuine grievance and reasonable claim for redress . . . . Isn't it time to deal seriously with the Palestinian question, instead of leaving it to the most irresponsible elements and the tactics of the madhouse?"

Africa, too, saw similar tragedies develop out of the failure of governments to respond to resistance movements. In Kenya, for example, Jomo Kenyatta, an English-educated African, led the Kenya African Union in nonviolent resistance to British rule. He appealed to the government in vain for reforms.

When he organized strikes, police suppressed them brutally. His request for fair representation of black Kenyans in the Legislative Council was rebuffed with the observation that natives would not be ready for self-rule for several hundred more years. Desperate Kenyans formed a terrorist band.

The Mau Mau made raids on settlements of whites and blacks who collaborated with the government, committing fearsome atrocities. Kenya was plunged into a bloodbath. Kenyatta was arrested and jailed as a suspected Mau Mau leader, although he had persisted in nonviolent resistance. In the end London was compelled to intervene, free Kenyatta and permit black Kenyans to vote for independence.

In the Belgian Congo (now called Zaire), the Congolese suffered for almost a century under the Belgians, who exploited them mercilessly for their rubber and other valuable natural resources. A strong resistance movement sprang up after World War II among young French-speaking high school graduates known as *evolués*, who held jobs as civil servants, teachers, craftsmen and white-collar workers. Forbidden to organize politically, they formed social, labor and tribal clubs.

They demanded equal pay with whites, improved opportunities, an end to racial discrimination, social welfare programs and a role in government. The Belgians introduced some reforms, but refused to share power with the blacks. Resistance leader Joseph Lumumba stirred crowds to demand self-rule. Riots broke out. The Bakongo tribe under Joseph Kasavubu began a campaign of civil disobedience.

The alarmed Belgian government, fearful that the Congo would fall into chaos and threaten its investments, agreed to elections in 1960 that led to an independent Congo Republic. But tribal rivalries and a lack of administrative knowledge plunged the new republic into turmoil.

The Belgians subsidized a secessionist government in Katanga under Moise Tschombe, an opportunistic black politician pledged to protect Belgian investments. For the next six years civil war raged in the Congo, worsened by foreign intervention.

Resistance tactics brought the Congolese independence but also anarchy. Resistance leaders learned that it was necessary not only to master the arts of successful protest but also to prepare themselves in the sciences of government.

Black governments showed that they could be even more ruthless than white colonial governments in suppressing black resistance. The Moslem regime in Nigeria, independent since 1960, refused to listen to appeals for self-rule in Biafra from the well-educated, successful Christian Ibo tribe.

Instead, the Moslems split Biafra into several states. When the Ibos united in resistance, they were slaughtered by Nigerian troops. Before they were forced to surrender in January 1970, they lost almost a million casualties.

In South Africa, where Gandhi's passive resistance movement was born, apartheid and racial oppression remained government policy. In the early 1950s a nonviolent civil disobedience campaign was led by the African National Congress (ANC). Blacks defied laws compelling them to carry curfew passes and forbidding them to trespass on white-only facilities. Many were punished by stiff fines, three-year jail terms and ten lashes with a whip.

One young black, jailed at hard labor for holding a protest meeting, described the treatment of ANC resisters in prison: "There was no heating, the cells were crawling with vermin and lice, and there was a perpetual stench . . . . We had to sleep on the floor, with no blankets, cramped against each other. At two A.M. the guard would yell in: 'You dogs still alive?' Then we were up at six to file out for breakfast—some cold yellow maize porridge in a zinc dish, which they flung at you . . . . In a week we'd become brutes."

The prisoners organized group resistance tactics, complaining to inspectors, getting too "sick" to work, using go-slow tactics on the job, and holding political discussions.

In March, 1960, the Resistance felt strong enough to call a mass rally at Sharpville in a show of civil disobedience. Police were notified in advance that no one in the crowds would carry the required curfew pass. On government orders, the police charged the crowd, firing repeatedly at unarmed men, women and children, killing 72 and wounding 180.

Outrage at the Sharpville massacre spread through all of Africa and the outside world. Black protest demonstrations erupted in several South African cities. Declaring an emergency, the white government outlawed all African political movements and arrested several thousand men and women. Whites who voiced resistance were placed under house arrest.

Deciding that peaceful resistance was no longer possible, many young Africans organized the Spear of the Nation, a guerrilla movement dedicated to violent acts of sabotage.

In 1972, when university students demonstrated against apartheid, Minister of Justice Petrus C. Pelser banned all marches and outdoor meetings. Police broke up meetings at Witwatersrand University and the University of Cape Town, arresting sixty-seven students. The Anglican bishop of Port Elizabeth held a multiracial protest rally of three-thousand people. Minister of the Interior Connie Mulder angrily warned churchmen to stick to "preaching the Gospel—and nothing else!"

The Reverend Theo Kotze refused. "The state has gone too far," he declared. "The time for truth to be spoken, loud and clear, has come." He was indicted on charges of "riotous assembly" for planning acts of civil disobedience.

The South African government's iron rule of terror has thus far prevented revolution. But the challenge of the Resistance has cost it world respect and barred it from the United Nations as a racist country.

Black resistance in neighboring Rhodesia caused England to order the white government to broaden voting rights, providing for eventual self-rule by the African majority. Prime Minister Ian Smith's refusal led to Rhodesia's expulsion from the British Commonwealth. And in May, 1968, the United Nations Security Council ordered a trade embargo against Rhodesia.

Hoping for a reconciliation through compromise, a British commission arrived in January, 1972. But black Rhodesians held angry protest demonstrations, compelling the commission to return home and report that the Resistance would accept no less than its original demands.

The Filipinos have long been addicted to resistance movements. They resisted Spanish rule, which the Americans helped them get rid of. When the Americans took over the islands in 1898 and tried to hold them, a resistance movement led by Emilio Aguinaldo forced Washington to promise the Filipinos independence. After the Japanese seized the islands in 1942, Filipinos organized a skillful resistance. Working with MacArthur's forces in the Pacific, they ended Japanese rule.

After Filipino independence in 1946, a new resistance movement was led by pro-Communist Huks, who demanded land, homes and rice for the peasantry. President Ramon Magsaysay, himself a former resistance leader against the Japanese, introduced sweeping liberal reforms that cut the ground out from under the Huks. Resistance ended, and the Huks dispersed.

In the intervening years an anti-American resistance movement has demonstrated repeatedly against two huge U.S. military bases kept in the Philippines by Pentagon subsidies to the Manila government.

In 1969 Senator Stuart Symington questioned a Pentagon spokesman: "In other words, we are paying the Philippine Government to protect us from the Philippine people who do not agree with the policies of the government or do not like the Americans?"

Lt. General Robert H. Warren replied, "To a degree, yes, sir."

Toward the end of 1972, the Resistance protested against widespread government corruption, high unemployment and the lack of land reform. Unrest swept the cities and the Moslem island of Mindanao. Declaring martial law, President Ferdinand Marcos arrested his political opponents and outlawed freedom of speech, press and assembly.

With all legal avenues of resistance closed off, thousands of workers and farmers went underground. In 1973 a new National Committee for the Restoration of Civil Liberties in the Philippines continued a three-century tradition of Filipino resistance against tyranny.

International resistance was aroused by two related postwar developments of the Cold War, the testing of nuclear bombs in the atmosphere, and the threat of atomic warfare. Both were seen as dangers to world survival.

In 1957, the Committee for Nonviolent Action (CNVA) held a vigil of seventy-five persons outside Nevada's atomic testing grounds. On Hiroshima Day, eleven tried to invade the test site "to present their bodies as a living barrier to the continuation of tests," and they were arrested for trespassing.

One year later CNVA consultant Albert Bigelow and four other pacifists, risking their lives in protest, attempted to sail a ketch, *The Golden Rule*, into a restricted zone of the Pacific where the H-bomb was to be detonated. Chased by the Coast Guard, they were stopped outside Honolulu, arrested and given two months in jail. Another CNVA yacht, *The Phoenix*, got sixty-five miles into the test zone before it, too, was stopped.

Sixteen CNVA members were arrested for invading the base at Mead, Nebraska, where intercontinental ballistic missiles were stored. Some went to jail for six months. The following year the CNVA picketed the boatyard building the nuclear submarine *Polaris*. One resister swam out to the nuclear sub *Ethan Allen* and boarded it illegally.

In the tense summer of 1961 that saw both the Soviet Union and the United States violate their moratorium on nuclear testing in the atmosphere, over five thousand students went to Washington to picket both the White House and the Soviet Embassy.

During 1962 another CNVA boat sailed to Leningrad to protest Soviet participation in the atomic race. Its members were not only denied port entry but also jailed.

Worldwide resistance organized by groups like the U.S. Committee for a Sane Nuclear Policy also put great pressure on the nuclear giants. Aroused public opinion compelled the United States and the Soviet Union to renounce testing in the atmosphere and any "first-strike" use of nuclear weapons. The Resistance also helped pressure the two governments into holding nuclear disarmament (SALT) talks to reverse the suicidal arms race.

7 Resisting the Iron Curtain

After World War II the Russians, whose armies had swept across East Europe to Berlin, imposed Communist regimes on the occupied countries they had liberated from the Nazis.

In Yugoslavia, however, a Communist regime was accepted by the people because it was led by Marshal Josip Broz Tito, the Marxist hero of the Resistance against the Nazi occupation. The Yugoslavs' faith in Tito as a patriotic leader was vindicated when he defied Stalin's attempts to control him, insisting that the Yugoslavs would find their own path to Communist goals, independent of the Kremlin.

Resistance movements against rule from Moscow sprang up in all the other Iron Curtain countries. But they were generally as powerless to win freedom as resistance movements under the Nazis had been. Their hopes were suddenly raised by an astonishing development in February, 1956, three years after Stalin's death, when Nikita Khrushchev made a three-hour speech to the twentieth Communist Party Congress denouncing the late dictator as a murderous tyrant.

The Resistance in Eastern Europe was quick to react. If Stalin was now conceded to have been a villain by the So-

viet Union itself, then why should Stalinist leaders in the
satellite countries be suffered in power? Especially since
Tito had shown that it was possible to defy the Kremlin
and get away with it, to the benefit of his own people.

Revolt was fanned by the broadcasts of Radio Free
Europe urging East Europeans to overthrow their Communist regimes. RFE was a Cold War propaganda agency
for which American contributions were raised to make it
seem a private venture. Actually, however, it received a
secret thirty-million-dollar CIA subsidy. "Wherever we
can," former CIA head Allen Dulles said later, "we must
help to shore up both the will to resist and confidence in
the ability to resist."

In October, 1956, long-smoldering discontent erupted in
Hungary. Several thousand university students staged
demonstrations demanding freedom of the press, a voice
in university affairs, and an end to required Marxist
courses. They were joined by workers demanding higher
pay and better working conditions. This unusual display
of open resistance behind the Iron Curtain frightened the
Hungarian Communist party into restoring to power a
popular former Premier, Imre Nagy, while calling upon
Soviet troops outside the city to restore order.

Meanwhile, on the evening of October 23, almost 300,000
Hungarians joined demonstrations outside the Parliament
building. It was a spontaneous uprising, with no central
leadership. "Our only general," cried one student, "is
general discontent!" A huge statue of Stalin was toppled
and smashed. The red star on top of Parliament was torn
down. A student delegation went to the radio station demanding that it be allowed to broadcast a manifesto of
resistance.

Hungarian security police arrested the delegation.
Tossing tear-gas bombs into the crowd, they opened fire,
killing several people. What had been largely a civil
disobedience demonstration now turned into bloody

rioting. Hungarian soldiers rushed to fight the demonstrators joined them instead.

Resistance had turned into revolution.

In the morning Soviet tanks, artillery and armored cars rumbled into the city. The crowds at first greeted them as friends, and the Russians were reluctant to fire on unarmed students and workers, even though their officers had told them that "Fascists" were trying to seize Budapest. But the wild firing of Hungarian plainclothesmen misled the Russians into thinking they were being ambushed by demonstrators. Their armored columns opened fire, strewing the square with bodies.

A shocked world outcry led the Kremlin to order Russian forces to withdraw from Budapest. But then Premier Nagy angrily informed the Soviet Ambassador that he intended to take Hungary out of the Warsaw Pact of Communist nations, declare neutrality in the Cold War, demand the withdrawal of all Soviet troops from Hungarian soil, and ask for aid from the Western powers and the United Nations. This defiance alarmed the Russians, who knew that any more dangerous examples like Tito could threaten the whole Communist alliance in East Europe.

Soviet tanks were ordered back into Budapest before dawn on November 4, 1956. Students attacked them desperately and were slaughtered. "It sometimes seemed that infants were in arms against armor," wrote *New York Times* reporter John MacCormac. "And there was that girl partisan who said, as she went out to fight, 'I am seventeen; I have lived long enough.'"

Hungarian soldiers joined the students in fighting the Russians from ambush. Although battles raged for several days, it was clear that the Nagy rebellion was doomed without outside help. A teletyped plea for aid went out to the West: "All Budapest is under fire. The Russian gangsters have betrayed us." But after all the Radio Free Europe broadcasts urging revolt, the West cautiously sent only sympathy.

The Russians replaced Nagy with hard-liner Janos Kadar as Premier, and by mid-November the fighting was over. More than 32,000 Hungarians had been killed, thousands imprisoned, and 175,000 more had fled the country as refugees.

Bitter Hungarian workers called a general strike. When the Russians threatened to smash any new demonstrations with tanks, the Resistance ordered all men to stay home. In their place fifty thousand women marched to the tomb of the Unknown Soldier, on the correct assumption that Soviet troops would hesitate to fire on a peaceful memorial march of women.

"It was the most beautiful sight I've ever seen," said one student rebel. "There was not a man in the streets. We watched from the windows as the women appeared from everywhere, walking in silence, with flowers in their hands to place on the tomb. The Russians made a circle of tanks around the tomb—and the women quietly climbed across them."

Many students felt that had the Resistance been able to keep civil disobedience nonviolent from the beginning, continuing its tactics of persuading Russian soldiers not to shoot at international comrades, the Resistance might have won.

From the day Soviet tanks entered Prague in May, 1945, as liberators, the Czechoslovakians began a resistance movement, caring no more for Russian rule than they had for Nazi rule. The Czechs were definitely Western-oriented. Youth resisted Soviet influence by an underground cult of playing and listening to forbidden Western jazz in Prague cellars. The Communist regime of Antonin Novotny constantly felt it necessary to send journalists to jail for "unpatriotic sentiments."

After Khrushev's denunciation of Stalinism, however, liberal Alexander Dubcek became influential in the Czech party Presidium. Under his pressure, Novotny made concessions to the Resistance. Western jazz, dancing and films were tolerated. Some Stalinist officials were fired. Attacks on liberal journals and writers subsided. Some imprisoned church officials were freed. Economic reforms were promised.

But the two wellsprings of the Resistance, writers and students, refused to be satisfied with only limited freedoms. In June, 1967, leading Czech writer Ludvik Vaculik told the Writers Congress, "Our republic has lost its good name."

His demand for total freedom of expression was suppressed by Czech police, who charged that the Writers Congress had been "masterminded by enemy agents in Paris."

Novotny expelled Vaculik and other dissident writers from the Communist party and put their magazine, *Literarni Noviny,* under direct government control. Czech writers promptly organized a boycott that drove its circulation down from 130,000 to just a few hundred.

That fall, Czech students, fed up with trying to study nights in unheated rooms with the lights turned off at 9 P.M., decided on civil disobedience of the law against unauthorized demonstrations. One night two thousand of them took to the streets of Prague carrying candles and chanting, "We want light!"

Startled, Novotny took the cry to signify a demand for uncensored news. Police squads broke up the demonstration by hurling tear gas and beating up young men and women indiscriminately. Next day government newspapers charged that "foreign agents" had organized the demonstration.

Angry students now broadened their demands to protest the whole political system, charging the Novotny regime with being stupid, inefficient, dishonest and repressive. Their resistance encouraged workers to make their own protest by organizing job slowdowns. The resistance movement grew rapidly, precipitating a struggle in the Communist Party between the conservative forces of Novotny and liberals led by Dubcek.

Dubcek won. On January 25, 1968, replacing Novotny as head of the Party, he declared, "We must remove . . . all the injustices done to people." Repudiating Novotny's harassment of writers and other intellectuals, he added, "We must eliminate everything that tends to hamstring scientific and artistic creation, everything likely to breed tensions." He promised new consideration for youth's demands, and called for developing "more, and above all, deeper democratic forms."

Czechs responded enthusiastically. A new day had dawned—perhaps even a return to democracy under Socialism. The Resistance rejoiced when Dubcek forced the Interior Ministry to apologize to students for police brutality. Workers were delighted when Dubcek fired Stalinist trade union bosses, paving the way for democratic choices. Government censors themselves now called for an end to political censorship.

The Resistance was allowed to hold public meetings denouncing the Novotny years. Newspapers exposed suppressed scandals of his regime. Prague Radio was turned over to liberals, who used it without censorship. It seemed impossible to dam up the rush of profound feelings being expressed by hundreds of thousands of Czechs who now felt truly liberated.

A delegation of five thousand young workers and students put on a demonstration in Wenceslas Square, snake-dancing and chanting slogans of the Resistance. They called upon Dubcek for a guarantee that the "bad old days" would not return. Coming out to greet them, he declared, "You yourselves are the guarantee—you, the young!"

On May Day, 1968, enormous crowds demonstrated in Prague in support of Dubcek. New signs appeared in their ranks: "Are six million citizens without a party worth less than a million Communists?" . . . "Free elections!" . . . "No more political police!" In a speech interrupted by deafening cheers, Dubcek promised to "make Socialism more attractive to the world."

The Kremlin grew deeply alarmed. Dubcek was obviously becoming another Nagy. The Resistance had won in Czechoslovakia and was now challenging Moscow's blueprint for Communist government. Deciding the time had come for a threatening display of Soviet power, the Kremlin staged Warsaw Pact military manoeuvers, a pretext for sending Russian troops into Czechoslovakia on May 30.

When Dubcek refused to be intimidated, the Russians sent a delegation under Leonid Brezhnev for a confrontation. Dubcek was accused of betraying international Socialism by working with Western "imperial interests." He argued that he simply wished "to create a Socialism which has not lost its human character." Appealing for popular support on television, he declared, "After long years of silence, each of us can express his opinion with dignity; Socialism begins to become the business of the whole people."

Czech scientists issued a statement called "Two Thousand Words to Workers, Farmers, Civil Servants, Scientists, Artists, and Everyone." Written by Ludvik Vaculik and signed by seventy leading Czechs, it called for a clean sweep of all Stalinists in office. "Let us demand the resignation of people who have misused their power . . . behaved dishonestly or cruelly," they urged. "We must find ways and means to induce them to resign— for instance, through public criticism, resolutions, demonstrations . . . strikes, boycotts." Pledging full support of Dubcek, they advised him, "Faced with superior Soviet forces, all we can do is remain politely firm and not start trouble."

"We have no other choice than resistance or capitulation," declared Jini Pelikan, head of Czech TV. " . . . . We would find new forms of passive resistance, but we would not surrender."

The infuriated Kremlin demanded that Dubcek crack down on the Resistance. But the Resistance flooded him with petitions signed by millions of Czechs, urging him to stand fast. When he did, the Russians accused him of involvement in a NATO plot to detach Czechoslovakia from the Warsaw Pact.

On August 20, 1968, Kremlin orders sent 700,000 Russian, Polish, Hungarian, Bulgarian and East German troops into Czechoslovakia. Branding the invasion illegal, Dubcek appealed to all citizens "to maintain calm and not to resist the troops, as the defense of our national borders is impossible at this time." He and other liberal Czech leaders were arrested.

The invasion and their arrests stirred a great spontaneous, nonviolent uprising. For a week after the tanks had rolled into Prague, crowds of Czechs argued with the invaders, some of whom thought they were in West Germany. The Czechs tried to shame them for using armed force against fellow Communists. Some students stood defiantly in front of Soviet artillery, baring their breasts. Scolding the Russians, the Czechs refused to obey their orders.

Journalists began to direct the Resistance through emergency military transmitters, which they also used to keep the outside world informed of developments. Czech railway workers delayed and sabotaged a train bringing in jammers to locate and stop the illicit broadcasts. Students and workers threw up street barriers, chalked freedom slogans on tanks, and changed traffic signs to confuse the invaders. Traffic police managed to delay and obstruct their columns. When the Russians sought to visit local Communist party meetings, Czech leaders abruptly read out final business and closed the meetings before the Russians could be seated.

The Russians sought a friendly word in vain. In Bratislava, capital of Slovakia, all conversation ceased when a Russian squad entered a bar. The squad leader invited the Czechs to "have a drink on us." They simply stared up at the ceiling. Unslinging his gun, he leveled it at the patrons and angrily ordered them to drink up. They drained the glasses silently, still staring at the ceiling. The chagrined Russians stalked out of the bar.

In Moscow, famous Soviet poet Yezgeny Yevtushenko sent a telegram of protest to the Kremlin: "I can't sleep. I can't go on living . . . . I have many personal friends in Czechoslovakia and I don't know how I will ever be able to look into their eyes if I should ever meet them again."

Stinging world criticism compelled Brezhnev to release Dubcek and his colleagues and recognize them as the legitimate Czech government. But Dubcek was forced to agree to the "temporary" Soviet occupation, to curb the Resistance press and radio, and to help restore order.

The "Prague spring" was over. In January 1969 a 21-year-old Prague student named Jan Palach set himself afire with gasoline in the center of Wenceslas Square to protest the Soviet occupation. His funeral turned into a new mass demonstration of Czech resistance.

When the Czech ice hockey team defeated a visiting Soviet team in March 1969, over 200,000 jubilant Czechs poured into the streets in a wild celebration. Burning red flags, they attacked the Soviet Aeroflot offices.

Charging a "counterrevolutionary plot," the Russians now replaced Dubcek with a hard-line Kremlin loyalist, Gustav Husak. Pro-Russian watchdogs were installed in each of thirty Czech daily papers, and pro-Russian writers took over control of the Writers Union. Conservatives were appointed to key positions in the Communist party. University faculties were purged, and the Students Union was dissolved.

On the anniversary of the Russian invasion, the Resistance mustered 100,000 Czechs who poured into Wenceslas Square in an anti-Soviet protest. They were dispersed by tear gas and truncheons. A *New York Times* headline reported: STUDENTS IN PRAGUE NOW KNOW THEIR "BEAUTIFUL DREAM" IS OVER.

The Husak regime purged over 250,000 people from the Communist party and professional organizations. Thirteen prominent Dubcek supporters were put on trial

for "sedition, slander of the republic and espionage."
Dubcek himself was reported to have suffered a nervous
breakdown after prolonged "interrogation" by a Party
commission.

Sir Basil Liddell Hart criticized the Czech Resistance for
its head-on tactics of strikes, confrontations and blunt defiance of the Russians. Slowdowns on the job, he suggested, are much more baffling and frustrating to an oc-
cupying power than open defiance, and can be sustained
for much longer. Pointing out that they had effectively
sabotaged German war needs during World War II in
Denmark and Norway, he observed, "There is usually no
answer to such go-slow tactics."

But the Czech Resistance had nevertheless united
students, intellectuals and workers in a common struggle
for freedom. It had given Czechs a taste of freedom for
eight months that would never be forgotten. And it had
exposed the Soviet pretext of altruistic friendship for cap-
tive countries behind the Iron Curtain, touching off
protests even in the Soviet Union itself. The Resistance
had cost the Kremlin dearly in terms of international
prestige and had brought charges of "Red imperialism"
from Communist rivals China and Yugoslavia.

In Yugoslavia the newspaper *Politka* declared, "Never
in the postwar period has the tragedy of a country so
deeply and so painfully shaken the world of our planet as
has the tragedy sustained by Czechoslovakia. Never
before was the world so united in the condemnation of
aggression."

In January, 1972, an underground group flooded factories with leaflets calling upon workers to boycott all official rallies of the Husak regime, oppose Husak bureaucrats in Party elections, and demand secret balloting.
Prague authorities announced that "a certain number" of
Czechs had been arrested for subversion. The flame of the
Czech Resistance still burns.

In 1964 liberal Communists in Rumania managed to win

Party control, and began resisting directives from Moscow. Three years later they defied Kremlin policy by establishing diplomatic relations with West Germany and by refusing to join Moscow in condemning Israel for the Arab-Israeli war. The following year they refused to join in the invasion of Czechoslovakia. In 1969 they even invited President Nixon to visit Rumania. It was the first visit by an American chief of state to an Iron Curtain country in twenty-four years, and they gave him an enthusiastic reception. Moscow accused Bucharest of "perfidy."

Nicolae Ceausescu, head of the Rumanian Communist party, also won friends in China by resisting the Soviet demand that Rumania agree to help defend Russia against any "attack from the East." Hard-liners in the Kremlin angrily called for "military maneuvers" in Rumania, but Brezhnev had learned the lesson taught him by the Czech Resistance.

In 1970 heavy floods in Rumania left 250,000 homeless and damaged over two million acres of farmland. Despite the need of Soviet aid, Ceausescu refused to yield to any of Moscow's political demands. The Chinese sent $400,000 in flood relief, and aid came from all over the world. The feeling of not standing alone buoyed the Rumanians in their continued resistance to Russian domination.

The Poles were grateful to be rid of the hated Nazis after World War II but soon demonstrated that they were not much fonder of the Russians. Polish resentment of Communist rule was expressed by overflow attendance in churches and in huge religious processions. In 1966 Communist party leader Wladyslaw Gomulka was infuriated when young Poles sang hymns outside his office, and sent police to club them away.

In 1967 he was forced to shut down a Warsaw play called *Dziady*, written in 1832, because audiences were stormily applauding such lines as "Polish history is conducted in a prison cell," and "Everyone sent here from Russia is

either a jackass, a fool or a spy." The play's ban provoked
a protest demonstration at Warsaw University, followed
by protests from the Writers Union against government
censorship.

Two university students were punished by expulsion.
When a demonstration of four thousand students demanded their reinstatement, steel-helmeted militia
violently dispersed them. Next day ten thousand furious
students took to the streets crying out for liberty and
constitutional rule. For a week, joined by young workers
and high school students, they battled militia and police,
who used clubs and tear-gas. Over twelve hundred were
arrested.

The students then shifted their tactics to passive
resistance—chiefly sit-ins and class boycotts. They kept
transistor radios tuned at top volume to broadcast
speeches by Dubcek from Czechoslovakia. Resistance
spread across the nation. City after city mounted
demonstrations of solidarity with the students. In Nowa
Huta, when steel workers joined student demonstrations,
police attacked them with water hoses, truncheons and vi-
cious dogs. More than a hundred were hospitalized.

Repression brought new waves of anti-Gomulka
demonstrations, which in turn brought new arrests, mass
expulsions from universities, and the firing of involved
students' parents.

The Resistance surfaced again in December, 1970, when
workers in port cities rioted against price hikes and wage
cuts right before Christmas. They were joined by a strike
of thousands of textile workers in Lodz. The uproar
mounted when several strikers were killed by police.

The Communist party was now forced to fire Gomulka
and replace him with Edward Gierek, whom the workers
trusted. He promptly cancelled the wage cuts and rolled
back prices.

Flushed with success, the Resistance continued to stage
mass meetings, slowdowns and work stoppages to
demonstrate Polish impatience with Communist rule.

"There is a different mood in Poland today," *Newsweek* noted in February, 1971. "After years of plodding stolidly to work and cautiously airing their grievances over vodka and beer with trusted friends and relatives, Polish workers are publicly letting off steam. Indeed, the entire nation has become a giant Hyde Park corner, where workers voice their opinions to anyone within earshot."

Gierek responded by introducing a new five-year plan to build better houses and manufacture more consumer goods, including a cheap "people's car." He also ordered all Party leaders to leave their desks and "get out and talk with the people," setting an example himself by spending time at factories listening to complaints. "Changes will be made," he promised.

"People have discovered that they can change things," observed a Gdansk journalist. "So they say that if what happened in December doesn't improve their lives, maybe they'll do it again."

8 "Madness" In Moscow

The Resistance against Stalinism began in February, 1956, when Nikita Khrushchev, the new Communist party boss in the Kremlin, made his startling denunciation of the crimes of Joseph Stalin's long reign as dictator. His exoneration of Stalin's victims reversed the whole thrust of Soviet policy.

"De-Stalinization" brought liberalization of Soviet civil and criminal codes, some liberty for dissent, concessions to the restless satellites in East Europe, and an attempt to better relations with the United States. After long years of repression, Khrushchev's renunciation of Stalinism and the thaw in the Cold War encouraged Russian intellectuals to make demands for freedom of speech, press and assembly.

When Khruschev realized that the reaction against Communist authoritarianism was going much further than he had intended, he grew alarmed and sought to curb all threats to Kremlin authority. He warned the Resistance in Hungary, Czechoslovakia, Poland and Rumania that when it came to "fighting imperialism"—a euphemism for crushing resistance—"We are all Stalinists!"

One of the first prominent Russians to feel the impact of Khrushchev's about-face was poet-novelist Boris Pasternak, whose novel *Dr. Zhivago* had been banned as subversive. When it was smuggled abroad and published, the Kremlin-controlled Russian Writers Union branded him unpatriotic and expelled him. In 1958 Pasternak was awarded the Nobel Prize for literature but was compelled to decline it.

A key figure in the Soviet Resistance was mathematician Aleksandr Solzhenitsyn, who had spent eight years in a Stalinist labor camp for writing a series of wartime letters to a friend in which he had criticized Stalin. Under Khrushchev he turned novelist and was permitted to describe his experiences in *One Day in the Life of Ivan Denisovich*, a searing indictment of the late dictator's prison camps.

The book created a sensation overseas and sparked a literary counterculture at home. More and more Soviet writers felt that they had not only a right but a duty to write truthfully about Soviet life, in spite of censorship.

Tolerance of the Resistance ended abruptly when Khrushchev lost power and was replaced by hard-liner Brezhnev. In 1965 the KGB (Russian secret police) arrested Andrei Sinyavsky and Yuri Daniel for spending manuscripts abroad for publication. Young Moscow writers and students who sought to demonstrate in their behalf were also arrested. In closed court, Sinyavsky was sentenced to seven years at hard labor, Daniel to five.

Brezhnev ignored protests from sixty-three Moscow writers, including Ilya Ehrenburg. To stop the Resistance at home and abroad that had developed under anti-Stalinism, he sought to rehabilitate the image of Stalin as a respectable hero of Soviet history. He was forced to abandon the plan when twenty-five leading Soviet figures, including nuclear physicist Andrei Sakharov, Bolshoi prima ballerina Maya Plisetskaya and Ivan Maisky, Russia's wartime ambassador to London, denounced it in an open letter.

KGB chief Vladimir Semichastny sought to purge fifteen hundred Soviet intellectuals he considered the backbone of the Resistance. He began by arresting Yuri Galanskov and three other journalists, who edited an underground magazine, for "anti-Soviet agitation." When sympathizers gathered in Pushkin Square to demonstrate in protest, they were also arrested.

Sakharov, a Nobel Prize winner, denounced the "crippling censorship of Soviet political and artistic literature." Semichastny accused him of heading a secret "anti-Communist front" of writers and intellectuals. But in 1967 the USSR was celebrating the fiftieth anniversary of the Soviet Revolution, and Brezhnev was anxious to avoid unfavorable publicity. Semichastny was removed as head of the KGB, and hints were dropped that Sinyavsky and Daniel might be quietly freed.

The Soviet Writers Union was allowed to hold its first Congress in six years. Solzhenitsyn, however, was denied the right to speak against the censorship that had "smothered, gagged and slandered" his second and third novels, *The First Circle* and *Cancer Ward*. In a letter of censure to the Union for its failure to defend over six hundred writers persecuted for their convictions, he wrote, "I propose that the Congress adopt a resolution which would demand and ensure the abolition of all censorship, open or hidden . . . . Will the Congress defend me? Yes or no?" The Union ignored his letter.

Smuggled out of Russia, it reverberated around the world as the voice of the Soviet Resistance. Over one hundred leading Soviet writers came to his defense, including Ehrenburg and Yevtushenko. The majority, however, cautiously agreed with Anatoly Kuznetsov, who said, "Solzhenitsyn is asking me to commit suicide with him." Most prudently stayed home from the Congress.

One of Solzhenitsyn's supporters, poet Andrei Voznesensky, was punished by cancellation of a trip to the Lincoln Center festival in New York City, where he had been invited to read his poetry. He wrote in outrage to *Pravda*, "I am a Soviet writer, a human being made of flesh and blood, not a puppet to be pulled on a string . . . . We are surrounded by lies, lies, bad manners and lies." When *Pravda* refused to publish his letter, he sent it abroad.

At a Moscow recital of his works, he read out an angry new verse: "They've taken out our sense of shame/ As an appendix is removed . . . ./ How shamefully we hold our tongues,/ Or at most we hem and haw." Summoned before the Writers Union, he was threatened with expulsion and blacklisting.

In subsequent weeks the Communist party expelled and fired from their jobs dozens of prominent writers, artists and historians who had protested the attempt to whitewash Stalin, the persecution of Solzhenitsyn, and the trials of writers.

At the trial of the Pushkin Square demonstrators, Vladimir Bukovsky defied the government after seven months in prison awaiting his day in court. "I absolutely do not repent of having organized the demonstration," he declared. "I believe it has done its job and, when I am free again, I shall organize other demonstrations!"

He was sentenced to three years at forced labor.

The Writers Union demanded that Solzhenitsyn repudiate his now-famous letter of protest published in the West. When he refused, his name was blacklisted in the Soviet press, all copies of *Ivan Denisovich* were removed from library shelves, and his subsequent books went unpublished.

When Galanskov was brought to trial in August, 1968, more than seven hundred artists, writers, scientists, sociologists and engineers signed petitions to the court protesting the proceedings as a "witch trial . . . no better than the celebrated trials of the 1930s which involved us in so much shame and blood that we still have not recovered." But Galanskov was sentenced to seven years at hard labor, his collaborators to five.

Noted mathematician Alexander Yesenin-Volpin denounced the verdict. He was seized, declared "mad," and forced into a mental institution. An immediate protest by ninety-five Moscow University mathematicians, who testified to his sanity, compelled the authorities to release him.

The Soviet invasion of Czechoslovakia shocked not only Russian intellectuals but a broad section of the people. Formal letters of protest were sent to the Central Committee by eight hundred Soviet organizations. A small demonstration was mounted in Red Square by physics instructor Pavel Litvinov and imprisoned Yuri Daniel's wife, Larissa. On a parapet in front of St. Basil Cathedral they unfurled homemade banners reading "Shame on the Occupiers!" "Free Dubcek!" and "Hands off Czechoslovakia!" They also displayed a slogan used by Polish rebels against Tsar Nicholas in 1830: "For your freedom and ours!"

Within minutes KGB plainclothesmen came running frantically from all over Red Square. "We sat quietly and offered no resistance," reported poetess Natalia Gorbanevskaya. "They tore the banners from our hands and beat Victor Feinberg on the face until the blood flowed, breaking some of his teeth. Pavel Litvinov was beaten on the face with a heavy bag. A small Czechoslovak flag was ripped from my hands and destroyed. They shouted: 'Get out of here, you scum!' We remained seated . . . . I was beaten up in a car."

Critic Victor Feinberg, badly disfigured, was sent to a mental hospital. The KGB also tried to confine Natalia Gorbanevskaya in an asylum, but the examining physician refused to find her insane because of her two small children. When she joined another protest demonstration, the KGB seized her again and this time made sure that the examining doctor confined her to a "special hospital for political insanity."

"We were able even if briefly to break through the sludge of unbridled lies and cowardly silence," she wrote in a letter smuggled out to the *New York Times*, "and thereby demonstrate that not all citizens of our country are in agreement with the violence carried out in the name of the Soviet people."

On the day after 21-year-old Jan Palach set himself afire in Prague to protest the Soviet occupation, a 22-year-old Leningrad Army engineering officer named Ilyin left for Moscow. During a motorcade for returning Soviet astronauts, he fired two pistols at a general he mistook for Brezhnev. Seized, he declared defiantly, "I did it to wake up Russia."

He, too, was confined to a mental asylum.

Lithuanian student Roman Kalanta imitated Jan Palach by setting himself afire in a Kaunus park, to protest Soviet religious restrictions. The tragedy drove several thousand youths into the streets shouting, "Freedom for Lithuania!"

Police and paratroopers clashed with the students. Protest leaders were arrested and sentenced to three years in jail. Police sought to minimize the Resistance as only a "few dozen drunken young rowdies . . . as a result of which public order was disturbed and traffic disrupted."

But despite a chain of arrests, the Resistance spread through Lithuania, Latvia, Estonia and the Ukraine, protesting forced Russification and political repression. In May, 1969, three officers of the Baltic Fleet and thirty civilians were arrested for forming a "union of fighters for political freedom" with branches in Moscow, Riga, Baku, Perm and Khabarovsk. Fifty members appealed to the U.N. Commission on Human Rights to stop "the unending stream of political persecutions in the Soviet Union, which we see as a return to the Stalin era."

At one trial in Kiev, the prosecutor demanded that defendant Boris Kochubievsky state whether it was true that Russians had fought the Nazis in World War II for freedom. Kochubievsky agreed. "Did we win?" The defendant again agreed. The prosecutor crowed triumphantly, "Well, there you are, then. So we *have* freedom!"

The controversy over Solzhenitsyn came to a head in November 1969 when he was expelled from the Writers Union for having permitted publication of his works abroad.

"It is time to remember that, above all, we belong to humanity," he protested, "and that man is distinguished from beasts by thought and speech; and that man by nature must be free. And if we are fettered, we return to a bestial state."

The Resistance circulated his banned works illegally in mimeographed editions. His expulsion was called "a crime against civilization" in a *London Times* letter signed by thirty-one distinguished international writers, who declared, "The treatment of the Soviet writers in their own country has become an international scandal." Bertrand Russell wrote Premier Aleksei Kosygin that Solzhenitsyn's blacklisting was "in the interest of neither justice nor the good name of the Soviet Union."

Playwright Arthur Miller protested for the worldwide writers' organization PEN. "We reject the conception that an artist's refusal to humbly accept state censorship is in any sense criminal in a civilized society."

But the Kremlin was far more worried about the Resistance than by international damage to Soviet prestige. In December, 1969, the editor of *Teatr* was fired for favorably reviewing a play on the abortive 1905 Russian revolution which made the point that any brutal repression of freedom is bad. Censors then shut down a play called *Watch Your Faces* because of references to the persecution of writers and intellectuals.

In February, 1970, four Western youths visiting Moscow distributed leaflets of protest outside a store. They were quickly arrested, and their leader, a 23-year-old Norwegian student, was sentenced to a year in a labor camp.

Distinguished biologist Zhores Medvedev indignantly denounced the government for censoring the mails to keep disapproved letters from Soviet scientists from reaching colleagues abroad. In May, 1970, he was arrested and hustled off to a mental institution. *The Chronicle of Current Events*, underground organ of the Resistance, aroused a storm of protest against his incarceration, compelling his release.

The official press heaped fresh abuse on Solzhenitsyn, who had joined the outcry. He was defended in an open letter to four Russian newspapers by famous cellist Matislav Rostropovich, who had given the novelist refuge in his country *dacha*. The authorities punished Rostropovich by forbidding him to play in a scheduled concert, but they relented when the other musicians refused to play without him. Instead, they forced him to cancel all concerts abroad.

Leningrad mathematician Revolt Pimenov was arrested for "not living right"—owning a collection of "anti-Soviet literature" which he lent to friends. He protested to Party secretary V. A. Medvedev that there was not a single line in any of his books undermining Soviet authority.

"For some time," he declared, "we scientists have lost our sense of personal security . . . . The threat to personal security explains the studying of politics. All this began with the trials of the writers . . . . The violation of legal rights drew attention to them and aroused public concern."

"If you think that we'll let everyone say and write just what they like," replied Medvedev, "that will never happen. We do still have enough power not to let people commit acts that will harm us. Never will there be any concessions at all in the sphere of ideology!" Pimenov was sentenced to five years in Siberian exile for "slandering the Soviet state."

This was the last straw for many Soviet scientists. Sakharov and eight colleagues organized a Human Rights Committee. Seeking to avoid arrest, they promised only "constructive criticism of the contemporary conditions of the system of legal rights of personal freedom in Soviet law." They urged the Kremlin to turn "toward democracy and freedom . . . soon—before Russia suffers disaster."

They were answered by Professor Grigory Deborin, who wrote, "Democracy is a class concept. The ruling classes use democratic institutions to preserve their domination . . . . The opinion is sometimes heard that it is 'undemocratic' to use force against slanderers and provocateurs, on the grounds that such people are merely expressing 'different views' . . . . In many countries a person may be brought to court for defamation of another. The state has an equal right to defend itself against slander and baseless allegations which undermine its prestige."

The Kremlin was angered in 1970 when the Nobel Prize for literature was awarded to Solzhenitsyn. "Deplorable!" declared the Soviet Writers Union. But thirty-seven Soviet intellectuals praised the award, in a statement given to Western correspondents in Moscow, while predicting Solzhenitsyn would suffer for it. "In our literature and art," asked cellist Rostropovich, "why do absolutely incompetent people so often have the last word?"

"There are men and women in the U.S.S.R.," noted an admiring editorial in the *New York Times,* "still willing to brave censure for their ideas and for free expression."

Solzhenitsyn was denied permission to go to Stockholm to receive the Nobel Prize, and Swedish officials were refused visas to come to Moscow and award it to him there. Solzhenitsyn asked the Swedish Academy to hold the award in trust for his son "in the event that my life is not long enough." The Soviet press burst into an orchestrated condemnation of all Soviet writers published abroad without official permission.

Soviet poet Iosif Brodsky, teaching at the University of Michigan after deportation as an "idler and parasite," declared bitterly, "They can take citizens in just two ways, either as slaves or as enemies. If you are not a slave, and yet not an enemy, they don't know what to do with you."

The Human Rights Committee kept spreading the message of the Resistance. "Now that I live for my principles," Sakharov told Western correspondents, "I find many friends, warm friends. Not among the big people but little people, real people." Socialism in Russia had proved a "grave disappointment," he added, which was why so many intellectuals were active in the Resistance. "These people have true courage," he said, "because, unlike me, the authorities have put them in prison."

He regretted U.S. President Nixon's visit to Russia. "The authorities seem more impudent because they feel that with detente they can now ignore Western public opinion, which isn't going to be concerned with the plight of internal freedoms in Russia."

Repression continued. Andrei Amalrik, a 32-year-old historian, was sentenced to three years in jail for his book *Will the Soviet Union Survive Until 1984?* Art critic Viktor Feinberg and engineer Vladimir Borisov were arrested for Resistance activities, declared insane and placed in a mental institution, where they went on a hunger strike. During an American lecture tour, when physicist Valery Chalidze criticized the Kremlin for refusing to respect Soviet constitutional guarantees, he was barred from returning home.

Government persecution was so relentless that in 1972 when the Resistance called a protest demonstration at Moscow's Pushkin statue to mark the thirty-sixth anniversary of Constitution Day, only twenty-five brave dissenters dared attend. They were far outnumbered by the police and secret agents who showed up. One activist said sadly, "Our struggle is nearly finished."

Can resistance work in a Communist dictatorship? The record is uneven. In the satellite countries it could not succeed, except for the brief Prague spring, in transforming a "dictatorship of the proletariat" into a Socialist democracy. But it did force change and reforms in most of the satellite countries, in order to prevent the possibility that mass resistance might escalate into full-scale revolution.

In the Soviet Union itself, the mechanisms of repression were so tightly organized that the leadership was largely sealed off from the masses. Resistance by intellectuals was contained in a political vacuum by censorship. The intellectuals were neither numerous enough nor organized enough to create an effective underground network for rousing the masses.

The Resistance was nevertheless able to bring about minor improvements in civil liberties. "The KGB doesn't torture people any more to get confessions," a Moscow dissenter told a *Newsweek* reporter. "When they question you now, they never lay a hand on you. In fact, the prisoner even has the right to ask for a lunch break."

But rigid control of the media succeeded in isolating the Resistance from mass support. This was the significance behind the unsuccessful struggle of Russia's intellectuals for freedom of the press. Andrei Sakharov admitted at the end of 1972 that their struggle had failed to force substantial change, but he insisted that the Resistance had to go on nevertheless.

"For us it is not a political struggle; it is a moral struggle," he explained. "We have to be true to ourselves."

9 Resisting Today's Dictators

When dictator Fulgencio Batista seized power in Cuba in 1952, the Cuban Federation of University Students staged four-day mock funeral ceremonies for the Cuban Constitution, which they literally buried in a coffin. They announced a boycott of classes until democracy was restored. Batista's reply was a military raid in which students were beaten, shot and killed. Shocked Cubans who protested were jailed and tortured.

Angry young lawyer Fidel Castro petitioned Cuba's Supreme Court to declare the Batista regime unconstitutional. The fearful Court refused, destroying Castro's faith in democratic procedures. When the graft-ridden Batista regime continued to torture and murder political opponents, Castro organized the Twenty-sixth of July Movement, a revolutionary underground.

Fighting guerrilla warfare against Batista's hated troops from the Sierra Maestra mountains, he was enthusiastically supported by Cuba's peasants and workers. After two years his forces overthrew the dictator. In 1959, as the new ruler of Cuba at thirty-two, Castro transformed the island into a Socialist state.

Spurned by the United States, he turned increasingly to the Soviet Union for aid and protection. Castro's pro-Communist drift alienated the Cuban middle class, which organized a new resistance movement, this time against him. But Cuba's peasants and workers, who had previously been paid only starvation wages when they had work at all, enjoyed far better lives under Castro and supported his regime.

Hundreds of thousands of middle-class Cubans emigrated to the United States. With American assistance and direction, the anti-Castro Resistance launched an ineffectual invasion of the Bay of Pigs. Instead of inspiring an uprising against Castro, it only rallied the people to his defense.

Why did the Resistance succeed against Batista and fail against Castro? The answer was simple. Castro had the basic ingredient Batista had lacked—popular support.

In one South American country after another supported by the United States, dictatorial governments have refused to heed their resistance movements, which consequently have turned revolutionary. Their police and military forces, trained by the CIA in counter-revolutionary tactics, have crushed guerrilla movements in Argentina, Brazil, Colombia, Ecuador, Paraguay, Peru and Venezuela.

The Resistance is strong in Brazil, where a wealthy three percent of the population owns sixty-two percent of the land. In 1964, the ruling military junta outlawed the National Students Union, jailed hundreds of labor leaders and banned strikes as "crimes against national security."

When the Resistance called a general strike in Osasco, police took over the city, jailing workers, searching churches and arresting priests. The Army hunted down and tortured peasant movement leaders. Two missionaries who had organized the building of a village school were arrested for "subversion," and their school was destroyed.

In 1968 popular indignation drove 100,000 Brazilians to protest in the streets of Rio de Janeiro. Some joined urban guerrillas in the underground Resistance. Like militant

Tupamaros in the police state of Uruguay, the Brazilian guerrillas kidnapped officials to force the release of forty political prisoners being tortured in the junta's jails.

Church resistance in Brazil is led by Dom Helder Câmara, Archbishop of Recife, who declares, "My manner of interpreting the Gospel leads me toward peaceful violence. But I accept all those who, in conscience, accept active violence . . . to do battle with the social disorder that keeps millions of human creatures living in subhuman conditions."

Marcio Moreira Alves, former member of the Brazilian Parliament and leader of the Catholic Left in exile, points out, "When all the established paths to change are barred, only the road of revolution remains open."

"Contemporary Spain provides a good example of a regime in which the scope of dissent is so limited that practically any form of open protest is illegal," observes Elliot M. Zashin in his book *Civil Disobedience and Democracy.*

Although the government of Generalissimo Francisco Franco was and is a repressive Fascist dictatorship, he could not completely repress the resistance movement. In 1962 workers at Bilbao defied a government decree outlawing strikes. When they laid down their tools to demand a living wage and the right to free labor unions, they sparked a massive wave of strikes throughout the Asturian mining areas.

Despite arrests and firings, the strikers' ranks held firm, supported by socially conscious young priests. The Catholic magazine *Ecclesia* defended their right to strike, and the Abbot of Montserrat declared, "The Church always speaks the truth. If this truth is not welcome to those that govern, then it is up to them to change things." Franco was forced to accede to some of the strikers' demands for union recognition and negotiation machinery. To save face, he fired two government officials responsible for provoking the strikes.

In 1964, university students demonstrated against government control of student unions. When police attacked them, thousands boycotted classes at the University of Madrid.

Two years later, 130 clerics marched in peaceful protest against police brutality toward imprisoned students. Police broke their ranks by clubbing, beating and kicking them. The Capuchin Monastery of Sarria was raided for sheltering 400 students who were organizing an independent student union.

Student strikes persisted in Madrid and Barcelona for the next three years but remained nonviolent. "What good would violence do?" asked one leader. "*They* have the power."

Students have forged an alliance with workers in a joint struggle for freedom from government control. Clandestine labor leader Ramon Marinez, a machinist twice jailed as a "dangerous Red," declares, "We are no longer alone." A whole network of sympathizers—lawyers, priests, sociologists, economists, small businessmen and even some officials—are supporting the Resistance.

"Most of them hold the political and social establishment in contempt as hypocrites and cynics whose spiritual development had been arrested in 1936," observed Franco biographer J. W. D. Trythall, "and who hoped to stop the clock at that date."

Franco declared a state of emergency in 1969. Under it, sweeping arrests were made for "illegal union activity." Priests who protested were arrested, beaten and tortured. In 1972, police arrested leaders of a Basque independence movement.

Franco's greatest weapon has been public dread of civil war, ever since the bloody holocaust he unleashed in 1936 to overthrow Spanish democracy. The Spanish people have no stomach for another such civil war as the price of getting rid of Franco. Most prefer to wait for his death and then move toward a free society peacefully, led by the Resistance.

The Resistance in Portugal is much milder because the dictatorship of Antonio de Oliveira Salazar was far less oppressive, like that of his successor, Dr. Marcelo Caetano. Travelers recently visiting Portugal, Madeira and the Azores found little discontent and a freedom to criticize the government as long as it was not done in public demonstrations or expressed in violence. "Violence," Salazar once said, "does not suit the gentleness of our temperament and customs."

But at the same time there has been no lack of violence in the government's efforts to stamp out the armed rebellion of natives seeking to free Portugal's African colonies.

A sensational act of resistance was carried out against Salazar by his political foe, deputy Henrique Galvão, from political exile. In 1961, to protest what he charged was a fradulent election, Galvão and twenty-four followers boarded the Portuguese liner *Santa Maria* at Curacao and seized it on the high seas. The ship's radio-telegraph was used to inform the world that the pirated ship was now "the first liberated portion of Portuguese territory."

For two weeks Galvão kept the Santa Maria at sea, dodging other ships and planes while he kept the radio-telegraph clicking with anti-Salazar propaganda. When he was satisfied that he had achieved his objective of directing world attention to his protest movement, he surrendered the ship at Recife, Brazil. He subsequently directed resistance activities for Portuguese political exiles from that country.

Greece has been a cockpit of resistance ever since the end of World War II. When the Nazis were forced out in 1944, British troops prevented the Resistance, which was Communist-led, from taking power. Instead they restored the Greek monarchy. The Resistance waged guerrilla warfare for two years until they were defeated by U.S. military aid.

In April, 1967, just before scheduled elections, a junta of Right-wing Greek Army officers under Colonel George Papadopoulos seized power "to save the nation from a Communist takeover." The junta established a military dictatorship with mass arrests, purges, martial law and censorship.

Mikis Theodorakis, the famous Greek composer, wrote poems, songs, political tracts and radio broadcasts protesting the torture of youthful prisoners by Papadopoulos' security police, until he himself was jailed.

The underground Resistance, known as the Patriotic Front, continued circulating his tracts and records. One of those arrested for it was actress Katerina Arseni, who was tortured, starved in a dungeon and threatened with execution.

"We couldn't lie down, we sat only with our knees up, the lack of air choking us, making us delirious and senseless," she reported. "Instead of falling asleep, we would fall into a coma." She eventually escaped and testified before the European Human Rights Commission in November, 1968.

Poet-archeologist Yiannis Leloudas was beaten and tortured but refused to betray other members of the Patriotic Front. He told his judges, "You say that it is only the Communists who are against you. I am not a Communist, and I am against you. It is precisely your kind, the Czars, the Batistas, the Chiangs, that bring Communism." He was sent to prison for life.

Arrested as chairman of a Resistance meeting, Father Petros Gavalas declared, "I hold it my duty to fight with all my powers against this harsh dictatorship which has been imposed on my beloved country." After twenty-seven days of torture, he lost his voice and hearing in one ear. Just before a scheduled visit of the European Human Rights Commission in March 1969, he was released with a warning not to testify under pain of death. He not only testified but one week later removed a photograph of Papadopoulos from a church and burned it in the courtyard as a profanation. He was swiftly rearrested.

Defying censorship, in March, 1970, twenty Greek intellectuals published an anthology attacking dictatorial oppression; three contributions were smuggled out of jail. Although the junta was not named directly, one editor wrote, "If you want to be effective in this type of resistance you must escalate. Otherwise you may find yourself helping the regime in its efforts to prove there is intellectual freedom there."

One poem read: "A government/ That fears/ Nothing else/ But the people/ Can hold out/ Precisely as long/ As the people/ fear nothing/ Else but/ The government."

Theodorakis believes that the Resistance would long ago have swept the Papadopoulos regime from power if it had not been for U.S. military aid. The Resistance accuses the CIA of having conceived the coup and sustained the plotters in order to keep Greece as a U.S. military colony and base.

In November 1969 the European Human Rights Commission found the Greek dictatorship guilty of torturing 213 political prisoners, at least five to death. To avoid expulsion from the Committee of Ministers of the Council of Europe, the Papadopoulos regime was forced to sign a pledge to respect human rights and permit inspection of prisons. However imperfectly observed, the pledge represented a triumph for the Resistance.

In the fall of 1972, Greece's eighty thousand university students demonstrated against the regime's rigging of student elections. The government drafted student leaders and sent club-swinging police on campus to beat up protesters. Students at the Athens Polytechnic went out on strike. One declared, "Two years ago, even one year ago, we were afraid of each other. There were government informers everywhere . . . . We now know that we are not alone. We are a movement."

A third of the population was still under martial law, with sixty constitutional safeguards suspended, by the spring of 1973. But the Resistance was growing steadily. Housewives began protesting rising food prices. Construction workers demanded higher wages. Bank employees warned the government to keep hands off their pension funds. Young workers returning from jobs elsewhere in Europe demanded comparable freedom.

"As the cruelty of this regime continues to show itself, the people will become more active," observed a 22-year-old philosophy student at the Athens Polytechnic. "Together we can restore parliamentary democracy to Greece."

Milovan Djilas, the right hand and old comrade of Marshal Tito of Yugoslavia, persistently criticized his country's Communist bureaucracy for sabotaging the Party's original goals of Socialism with democracy. In 1954 he was stripped of all his offices and retired to private life. Continuing to blast the Yugoslav Communist party as "reactionary" and "Stalinist," he even criticized Tito in 1956 for not having condemned Khrushchev's armed intervention in Hungary.

Djilas and Tito together had courageously resisted Stalin's insistence that Yugoslavia must become a Soviet puppet. Their defiance had succeeded in preserving their country's independence. Now Djilas, ironically, was showing the same resistance to Tito, who reluctantly permitted the bureaucracy to jail him for "slandering Yugoslavia."

Djilas continued his resistance from prison, writing a book detailing his charges against the Communist bureaucracies of both Yugoslavia and the U.S.S.R. It was smuggled abroad for American publication. Wanting to free his old friend, Tito begged Djilas to recant. When Djilas refused, Tito paroled him anyway in 1961. The determined Djilas promptly published another book that embarrassed now-mended Soviet-Yugoslav relations. The Party uproar forced Djilas back to jail for "disclosing official secrets." Djilas supporters began publishing articles overseas in his defense.

The Resistance was led by young Mihajlo Mihajlov, an admirer of Solzhenitsyn. When he tried to publish a magazine in Zagreb, Mihajlov was arrested and the project blocked. Paroled until trial, he refused to flee. "If I am convicted," he declared, "then the authorities will be admitting that they identify Socialism with a single-party system."

He was sent to jail for a year for "defaming Yugoslavia's Communist society at home and abroad." Soon after his release, he was arrested again for smuggling out new articles attacking the bureaucracy and was jailed for three more years.

In 1966, after Djilas had been in prison for five years, Tito finally persuaded the YCP to free him. Djilas promptly praised Mihajlov and continued to criticize both the YCP and the Soviet Union. He expressed some criticism of Tito as well but also praised him as a great Yugoslav patriot.

Because of Tito's personal regard for democracy, Yugoslavs found it easier to organize resistance to their Communist bureaucracy than dissidents in other Communist countries. In 1968, when student revolt swept the Western world, the universities of Yugoslavia also erupted in demonstrations against the status quo. Angry YCP officials urged a get-tough policy, but Tito went on radio and TV to acknowledge the justice of student complaints. Promising to meet their demands with reforms, he granted amnesty to those arrested during the demonstrations and pledged that those officials who had been responsible for police brutality would be dismissed. He even blamed himself and YCP leaders for having failed to resolve social problems that had troubled Yugoslavs for years.

"I promise the students that I will devote all my energies toward solving their problems," he declared. "If I am not capable of solving [them], I will resign from my post."

This gratifying response to the Student Resistance won
Tito a roaring ovation on every Yugoslav campus. "Tito is
with us and we're with Tito!" students shouted. Next day
they returned quietly to their classes.

In 1973 the Soviet Union, which had once blasted Tito as
an "imperialist spy, coward and bankrupt Fascist traitor"
for his resistance to Stalin, pretended it had never said
such things and urged Norway to consider Tito as the
logical choice to be awarded the Nobel Peace Prize.

In China, until 1949 the corrupt, dictatorial government
of Chiang Kai-shek's Kuomintang, supported by the
United States, refused to make any reforms demanded by
China's middle class. This resistance movement then
joined forces with Mao Tse-tung's Communists. When
Japan invaded China, the Resistance insisted that Chiang
fight the Japanese with a Popular Front coalition.

But Chiang had an alliance with China's wealthy
bankers and industrialists. Instead of fighting the
Japanese, he used American arms and money to fight the
Communists, forcing them into civil war. During World
War II, the masses of Chinese joined the anti-Japanese,
anti-Kuomintang Resistance. The end result was Chiang's
overthrow in 1949 and the establishment of Mao's People's
Republic of China.

Ironically, in 1966 Mao felt that a bourgeois Resistance
against his revolutionary ideas was developing among
Party and government officials, to the extent that power
was slipping from his hands. He decided to reestablish his
dominance and purge the Resistance by calling out the
nation's youth from schools and colleges. Organizing the
"Great Proletarian Cultural Revolution," he sent a force
of fourteen million young Red Guards fanning out through
the country to harass, attack and humiliate bureaucrats
and others in high places who failed to endorse the
"Thoughts of Chairman Mao."

The bourgeois Resistance fell apart under this on-
slaught. But so, almost, did the Chinese Republic. When
Mao finally called off his GPCR, it took months for the
country to recover normal operating efficiency.

An underground Resistance still operates. "In the country, the rebel organizations, disillusioned by the trend toward military rule, have not disarmed," reported W.A.C. Adie, British Foreign Office expert on Far Eastern affairs, in 1969. "Some have established sophisticated underground liaison systems. Some have adopted openly anti-Maoist positions, calling for a 'new socialism' or a 'second cultural revolution to overthrow the Communist Party.' Others still wave the red flag to oppose the red flag."

Despite all the repressive machinery at their disposal, today's dictators on both the Right and Left have not been able to stamp out the Resistance, and they probably never could.

10 Resistance
In Vietnam

The Vietnamese are a people with a long history of resistance against foreign invaders. They drove invading imperial Chinese forces out of Vietnam five different times between 40 A.D. and the fifteenth century. Resistance began again when the French made themselves colonial masters of all Indochina in 1884. But it was harder to get rid of a strong Western power with a formidable navy and army.

The struggle against French rule was led by Ho Chi Minh, a Communist leader who founded the Vietminh, the League for the Independence of Vietnam. When the Japanese seized Vietnam at the outset of World War II, Ho forged a united front of all political parties dedicated to a nationalist struggle against both the Japanese and their Vichy French puppets.

Ho cooperated closely with the American OSS, supplying them with military intelligence, sabotaging Japanese and Vichy forces, and rescuing Allied pilots shot down over Vietnam. OSS commandos who parachuted into Ho's headquarters lived and worked closely with him, supplying the Resistance with small arms used in raids on the Japanese.

The Japanese unleashed a savage reign of terror against all Vietnam civilians suspected of being Vietminh. But the people remained fanatically loyal to "Uncle Ho," even after Japan set up a Vietnamese puppet in Saigon, Emperor Bao-Dai.

With the Japanese defeat, the French under Charles de Gaulle were determined to regain Indochina as a colony. President Franklin Roosevelt, strongly opposed to colonialism, had planned to make it a U.N. trusteeship. When his death elevated Harry Truman to the Presidency, however, Truman backed the French as they seized power again in Southeast Asia as a "bulwark against Communism."

Charging betrayal, on September 2, 1945, Ho proclaimed the establishment of a Democratic Republic of Vietnam. At its capital in Hanoi, he read a Declaration of Independence based on the American document. "A people who have courageously opposed French domination for more than eighty years," he insisted, "a people who have fought side by side with the Allies against the Fascists during these last years—such a people must be free and independent."

He denounced the French who had reestablished themselves in the south: "They have built more prisons than schools. They have mercilessly slain our patriots; they have drowned our uprisings in rivers of blood . . . .They have fleeced us to the backbone, impoverished our people, and devastated our land. They have robbed us of our rice fields, our mines, our forests, and our raw materials . . . . The whole Vietnamese people, animated by a common purpose, are determined to fight to the bitter end against any attempt by the French colonialists to reconquer our country!"

For the next nine years Ho led a fierce resistance against the French. He appealed for help to Washington, but the French persuaded Truman that Ho was just a stalking horse for the Red Chinese—part of a plot to put all Southeast Asia under their control. Truman provided the French with hundreds of millions of dollars' worth of

arms and supplies to crush Ho's Democratic Republic in
the north.

Forced to abandon the cities, Ho took his government
and guerrilla forces into the countryside, fighting the
French from the midst of the peasantry. So successful was
the Resistance that the United States felt compelled to set
up a Special Forces unit in 1952 to train, direct and arm
native mercenaries as a counter-resistance. But the
Vietminh had total popular support, and the French
continued losing despite a forty percent superiority in
fighting manpower and a thousand percent superiority in
fire power.

At Dienbienphu in 1954, Vietminh General Vo Nguyen
Giap set a trap into which the French Army stumbled.
Facing total annihilation, its generals frantically appealed
to President Dwight D. Eisenhower for American intervention to save them. The United States was already
paying eighty percent of the war's cost.

Secretary of State John Foster Dulles wanted to bomb
North Vietnam with atomic warheads. Vice President
Richard M. Nixon supported a plan of Admiral Arthur
Radford to send three hundred fighter bombers. General
MatthewRidgeway opposed intervention.

Eisenhower agreed. A general who hated war, he
was reluctant to allow the United States to be dragged any
further into a bloody colonial war that he knew could end
only with American troops bogged down in land fighting
in Southeast Asia. He recognized that the conflict was
basically a political one and that the Vietnamese people
supported Ho and the Vietminh as the patriotic forces of
independence.

So he refused to intervene, advising the French to ne-
gotiate for a peace settlement. The result was the Geneva
Accords, signed at Geneva on July 20, 1954, by the
Vietminh and the French, and approved by Britain, the
Soviet Union, Cambodia, Laos and the French puppet
regime of Bao Dai in Saigon.

The settlement ended the war and divided Vietnam into two *temporary* zones at the seventeenth parallel. Countrywide elections were to be held in two years under the supervision of an International Control Commission (ICC), and would decide a unified government for all Vietnam. Meanwhile Ho would govern the north and the French the south, through Bao Dai.

Dulles, pressed by the United Nations to announce American acceptance of the Accords, issued a guarded statement "noting" the Geneva agreement and promising that the United States would "refrain from the threat or the use of force to disturb" the settlement. But he was already determined to undermine the Accords by freezing the two temporary zones into a permanent arrangement, turning the south into an American puppet state. Central to his plan was sabotage of the elections scheduled for 1956.

"I have never talked or corresponded with a person knowledgeable in Indochinese affairs," Eisenhower admitted later in his biography, *Mandate For Change*, "who did not agree that had the elections been held as of the time of the fighting, possibly eighty percent of the population would have voted for Ho Chi Minh." Secretary of State Dulles was determined to see that they never got the chance.

He forced the French to replace Bao Dai with his own choice, an anti-Communist Catholic politician, Ngo Dinh Diem, whom he could trust to organize a pro-American "government" of South Vietnam. The imposition of Diem on the ninety percent Buddhist population only intensified opposition. The southern Resistance was led by the Communist Viet Cong, supporters of Ho's northern Vietminh.

To crush them the United States sent Military Assistance Advisory Groups and American arms to Saigon. CIA advisors trained Diem's secret police, palace guard and Army officers. The secret police spread terror by fingerprinting the population. Dissenters, political rivals and Viet Cong suspects were arrested and tortured in concentration camps. Diem ordered all suspects shot on sight and offered rewards to all informers who betrayed members of their families as Viet Cong.

During the first five years of his regime, Diem arrested or murdered 150,000 political opponents and liquidated tens of thousands of others who demanded that the Geneva Accords be implemented. Praised by U.S. officials in Saigon for achieving "order and stability," Diem refused to allow the ICC to investigate his atrocities and treaty violations.

The CIA sent "pacification" teams around the southern countryside in a vain attempt to persuade the people to trust Diem. Backed by a billion dollars in U.S. military and economic aid between 1955 and 1960, Diem staged demonstrations against the Geneva Accords and the scheduled elections. His agents burned the hotel lodging the ICC commissioners in Saigon. Diem then refused to allow the elections to be held because he personally had not signed the Accords.

Dulles supported his violation of the Accords, declaring that the United States now regarded South Vietnam not as a temporary zone but as a separate nation. To provide a pretext for such recognition, Diem staged a rigged election in the south. Even though the press was censored, rivals were jailed and anti-Diem voters were threatened, he got less than a third of the votes. Foreign correspondents laughed when he was declared "elected by a plurality of ninety-eight percent."

Three days later, Diem proclaimed his own "Republic of Vietnam." Stung by U.S. press criticism, the CIA tried to get him to permit some token political opposition, but Diem flatly refused. He ran South Vietnam as a tight dictatorship.

With American help he created a "Civil Guard" of forty thousand militia to "pacify" the countryside. Village councils were overthrown, replaced by Diem's henchmen. Villages offering resistance were shelled by artillery and their residents arrested. Hated landlords driven out by the Viet Cong returned with the Civil Guard to claim back their lands and collect exorbitant rents and taxes. Millions of Vietnamese in the south who had not been Communists joined the ranks of Viet Cong guerrillas, especially in the Mekong Delta.

"The insurrection existed before the Communists decided to take part, and they were simply forced to join in," observed French historian Philippe Devillers. "And even among the Communists the initiative did not originate in Hanoi, but from the grassroots, where the people were literally driven to take up arms in self-defense."

In 1958 some of the young men of the south who had gone north after the Geneva settlement began returning home, now trained in Communist techniques of radio communication, ordnance repair, sabotage and propaganda. By the end of 1960, it was estimated that about forty-five hundred had returned to join the growing bands of Viet Cong. Diem and the United States accused "North Vietnam" of invading "South Vietnam," in violation of the Geneva Accords Saigon and Washington had sabotaged.

Ho Chi Minh dryly asked how Vietnamese returning home could be accused of invading their own country. The only foreigners in the south, he pointed out, were Americans.

By early 1959, the Resistance in the southern countryside was so widespread that Diem was forced to establish drumhead courts sentencing to death Vietnamese only suspected of being Viet Cong. The CIA resettled whole villages in fortified zones to try to isolate the Viet Cong from peasant support. The Viet Cong struck back by assassinating fourteen hundred Saigon-appointed village officials and kidnapping seven hundred others.

Much of the huge amounts of American aid sent to Saigon ended up in the pockets of Diem's family, corrupt officials and Army officers. By April 1960 his regime was so widely detested that even eighteen conservative South Vietnamese nobles, including former ministers, signed a public statement accusing him of operating a corrupt bureaucracy. Pointing out that he had filled the prisons with political prisoners, they predicted "soaring waves of hatred and resentment of a terribly suffering people standing up to break their chains."

One group of discontented young army officers rose in revolt in November 1960. Thousands of civilians joined them in a march on Diem's palace. Diem's troops crushed the uprising, killing four hundred rebels. One month later, the Resistance formed a United Front coalition consisting of the National Liberation Front (NLF), the Viet Cong, Buddhist groups, moderate and liberal politicians, young Army officers and non-Communist peasant leaders. Viet Cong forces were augmented by peasants who farmed by day and fought by night.

President John F. Kennedy, who had been humiliated by the failure of the Bay of Pigs invasion of Cuba, felt that he could not afford a fresh military disaster in Vietnam. He increased Diem's U.S. military "advisors" to twenty thousand. Seeking to undercut the Resistance, he demanded that Diem immediately introduce sweeping land reforms, restore free speech and democracy, release political prisoners and end corruption.

Diem flatly refused. Ho Chi Minh charged that American forces were now fighting beside the ARVN. The Pentagon denied it until U.S. newsmen reported that they were leading units in combat and flying helicopters and planes. The Pentagon then admitted it, but insisted that the Americans were only acting in "an advisory and training capacity."

To equalize the buildup of American arms and military specialists in the south, Ho sent North Vietnamese arms and military specialists to the NLF over the "Ho Chi Minh Trail" on the western border of Vietnam.

The Diem regime grew steadily more repressive. American correspondents saw villagers beaten, kicked, tortured and drowned to make them inform. Newsmen who reported these atrocities were ordered out of the country by Diem.

In May, 1963, when Buddhists in Hue demonstrated against Diem, he sent troops who banned speeches and threw hand grenades into the peaceful crowds, killing nine teen-agers, mostly girls. Hundreds of university students joined priests in the pagodas to protest by hunger strikes. They were dragged off to jail, and U.S. newsmen covering the event were beaten by Diem's police. Over forty Hue University professors resigned, and anguished Buddhist priests began setting themselves on fire in public squares as sacrificial protests.

In August Diem's police and troops broke into pagodas all over the south, beating helpless monks and nuns with rifle butts, and arresting Buddhist leaders. When students at Saigon University threatened to strike, four thousand were arrested and Diem closed all schools and universities. The arrival of a U.N. fact-finding mission was greeted by another monk who set himself ablaze before Saigon's Catholic cathedral.

A young Buddhist priest was asked how he justified such grotesque acts of resistance. He replied, "The Buddhists tried fasting, and processions, and sit-downs. But the police came to beat them and take them to prison. Burning was a final way—a reluctant way." It did not move Diem, but it grieved the people and appalled the American President.

Kennedy accused the Diem regime of having "gotten out of touch with the people." But it had never been in touch with them from the first. The CIA recognized that the Resistance would soon escalate into revolution if Diem did not fall. A group of military conspirators was allowed to understand that Washington would not be unhappy about a coup d'etat.

On November 1, 1963, a sudden Army putsch overthrew Diem, who was shot "while trying to escape." The United States quickly recognized the new military regime in Saigon. But the Resistance now had such support that over the next eighteen months ten different Saigon regimes failed to win the people's confidence. No matter who was in power, talk of negotiations or peace with Hanoi remained a prison offense, and the jails overflowed with political prisoners.

In 1964 fully 100,000 troops of the 300,000-man ARVN Army resisted the Saigon regime by deserting. President Lyndon B. Johnson came to the conclusion that if there was to be a military victory in Vietnam to save face for the United States, which had become hopelessly involved and compromised, it would have to be won with American troops.

As his pretext for intervening with over half a million U.S. soldiers, an American fleet and an armada of bombers, Johnson alleged that Hanoi PT boats had made attacks on U.S. ships in the Gulf of Tonkin. Congress passed a "Gulf of Tonkin Resolution" authorizing the President "to take all necessary measures to repel any armed attacks against the forces of the United States and to prevent further aggression."

Senator William Fulbright later accused the Defense Department of having wilfully invented the alleged attacks, as testified by sailors abroad the U.S. ships.

Over a million Vietnamese were estimated to have perished under heavy American bombing raids on both North and South Vietnam. U.S. battle deaths exceeded forty-five thousand, with over a hundred thousand wounded. But nothing shocked the American people like revelations of terrible massacres of helpless civilian men, women and children by U.S. troops who burned suspected Viet Cong villages and executed their inhabitants.

Although the Saigon regime was stabilized under the dictatorship of Nguyen Van Thieu, he could no more command the loyalty or support of the South Vietnamese than his predecessors. The jails once more overflowed with political opponents; the press was censored; NLF prisoners were kept in torture cages; corruption remained the order of the day.

In the north, Ho Chi Minh declared, "We will never sur-render our independence to purchase peace with the United States." His people toiled day and night under daily American bombings to repair bridges, roads and fac-tories destroyed by the raids. They built factories in countryside caves. In underground quarters, young workers operated lathes and drill presses, and medical schools trained corps of doctors and nurses. Rice mills were operated by women workers who kept rifles on window sills to fire at raiding American planes.

French journalist Michèle Ray was captured by the Viet Cong and traveled with them. She reported that she found Resistance fighters and their families "apparently in fine shape and with an excellent morale, a people living under incessant bombardments, who can laugh, joke, and go on living."

An Atlanta infantry major named Beckwith admitted to U.S. newsmen that the VC were "the finest soldiers I have ever seen in the world except Americans . . . . I wish we knew what they were drugging them with to make them fight like that. They are highly motivated and highly dedi-cated."

The American antiwar Resistance finally compelled President Johnson to stop the bombings and offer peace negotiations. But the peace talks dragged on endlessly, even through the first four years in office of Richard Nixon. Expanding the war into Laos and Cambodia, Nixon dropped more bombs on North Vietnam than were drop-ped in all of World War II and also mined the harbor at Haiphong. He sought to extricate U.S. troops by withdrawing them slowly as he "Vietnamized" the war by replacing them with U.S.-trained ARVN troops.

A "stand-in-place" ceasefire agreement was finally reached with North Vietnam on January 27, 1973, whereby the United States agreed to withdraw all military forces in Vietnam, in exchange for American prisoners. Hanoi was permitted to keep over 125,000 troops in South Vietnam, a point insisted upon by the North Vietnamese to emphasize that there was only one Vietnam, not two. A number of released U.S. prisoners accused the North Vietnamese and Viet Cong of having tortured them to make anti-American statements.

No longer propped up by U.S. military forces, Thieu tried to give the impression of popular support by hiring "rent-a-mob" South Vietnamese to throw rocks at Communist headquarters in Hué. "Saigon insisted that the attacks were spontaneous demonstrations," observed *Newsweek* in March, 1973, "but U.S. officials readily conceded that they were staged assaults."

It seemed incredible that a tiny little country like North Vietnam could have withstood for so long the terrible pounding it took from the air and the sea by the greatest military giant in the world, with no air or sea power of its own to reply with. Only the firm resistance of the Vietnamese people to foreign intervention—a resistance with a heritage of almost two thousand years—bonded them in the determination to drive invaders off their soil and unite all of Vietnam under one government, freely elected with international supervision, as had been promised them in the Geneva Accords of 1954.

One secret strength of the Vietnamese people was their knowledge that the American people would not indefinitely tolerate an unjust and immoral war of genocide against them.

They were proved right by an American antiwar movement that shook the United States as never before in its history.

11 "Stop the War!"

When President James Madison demanded a draft for the War of 1812, Daniel Webster thundered, "Is this, sir, consistent with the character of a free government? Is this civil liberty? . . . . Where is it written in the Constitution . . . that you may take children from their parents . . . and compel them to fight the battles of any war in which the folly or the wickedness of the government may engage it?"

Many thousands of Americans since have agreed with Webster and have gone to jail for their beliefs. In 1969, when Quaker Bob Eaton was sentenced to three years for resisting the draft, it was his sixth jail term for social protest. Speaking for the Committee for Nonviolent Action, he said, "We feel we should go back to the old days when Friends weren't afraid to challenge the government and go to jail for their convictions. We believe in noncooperation with unjust laws."

The anti-Vietnam Resistance began in 1964 with youths in the May Second Movement, who coined the slogan "Hell, no, we won't go." But they, the Student Peace Union, the War Resisters League and the Quakers represented only a tiny minority of Americans. The vast majority believed in "standing behind the President" in Johnson's decision to escalate the war.

Tried for draft resistance in 1965, nineteen-year-old Tommy Rodd told the court, "I am forced by my conscience to stand as representative of the suffering millions of Vietnam. I am forced to stand for the girl child burned to death in Bien Hoa, for the refugee cold and hungry in a camp on the outskirts of Saigon . . . for the thousands with no legs, thousands more with no eyes . . . . My word from them to this government, to this country is this: 'Stop this war!' "

He was sentenced to four years in Federal prison.

Universities held mass "teach-ins" to protest the war. Yale Professor Staunton Lynd drew stormy applause when he told Berkeley students, "I am advocating nonviolent retirement of the present Administration, that is, the creation of civil disobedience so persistent and so massive that the Tuesday lunch club which runs this country—Johnson, Rusk, McNamara, Bundy—will forthwith resign . . . . We must vote with our feet by marching and picketing; if necessary vote with our backsides by sitting in jail . . . . Thoreau said that one man ready to die could stop slavery in America. I think all of us here this weekend should . . . stand in front of the flamethrowers, and say: 'If blood must be spilt, let it be mine, and stop killing Vietnamese children. If you must search and destroy, let me save you the trouble—here I am!"

The first antiwar march on Washington was organized by the Students for a Democratic Society (SDS) in April, 1965. Over twenty thousand demonstrators picketed the White House, held a rally at the Washington Monument, then marched four abreast from the Mall to the Capitol singing "We Shall Overcome."

Recognizing that intellectuals were the backbone of the Resistance, President Johnson sought to cajole them into muting their opposition by putting on a "White House Festival of the Arts." Poet Robert Lowell declined his invitation in an open letter to the President on the front page of the *New York* Times. "The strangeness of the Administration's recent actions," he wrote, filled him "with the greatest dismay and distrust."

Many other prominent intellectuals refused to attend the Festival. Lewis Mumford, President of the American Academy of Arts and Letters, said that artists and writers had "a special duty to speak out openly in protest . . . [against] our government's cold-blooded blackmail and calculated violence." Artist Jack Levine declared, "I believe it is impossible to divorce U.S. culture from our policies in Vietnam, and I think our policies in Vietnam are appalling."

Author John Hersey accepted his invitation to read a selection from his books. But the selection, he announced, would be from *Hiroshima*, a passage that stressed the horrors of America's use of the atom bomb against Asians.

Infuriated, Johnson told his special consultant, Professor Eric F. Goldman, that he had had "enough of these people." He complained, "Some of them insult me by staying away and some of them insult me by coming . . . . Don't they know I'm the only President they've got and a war is on?"

He angrily refused to attend the Festival himself, substituting his wife to save face. The First Lady insisted that John Hersey must not read aloud from *Hiroshima*. "The President is being criticized as a bloody warmonger," she told Goldman. "He can't have writers coming here and denouncing him in his own house, as a man who wants to use nuclear bombs."

"The President and the White House are symbols of freedom," Goldman replied. "It is not freedom to tell this author what he can and cannot read." Hersey won his way, but the President banned press coverage of the Festival.

When youths began burning draft cards at antiwar rallies in front of television cameras, Senate hawk Strom Thurmond whipped a bill through Congress providing five years in prison and a ten-thousand-dollar fine for burning a draft card or inciting the act.

"It wouldn't be so bad if these people didn't make a public protest with their cards," Senator Everett Dirksen said on TV, "but just went out behind the barn and burned them."

The American Civil Liberties Union called the bill unconstitutional, holding that it violated the right of free speech. Burning a draft card was simply a symbolic way of dramatizing a protest against injustice.

In November, 1965, Baltimore Quaker Norman Morrison set himself aflame a hundred yards from Secretary of Defense Robert McNamara's office window in the Pentagon, in a desperate attempt to bring home to the American people what they were doing to Vietnamese men, women and children with napalm. A Hunter College student immolated himself in a similar tragic protest one week later. Shock waves ran through the public.

The next month, Yippie leader Jerry Rubin led a demonstration in San Francisco against General Maxwell Taylor. Sentenced to a month in jail, he shouted in the courtroom, "Our act was a political protest. Our punishment is political. We are today political prisoners."

At the same time thirty-five University of Michigan students organized a sit-in at the Ann Arbor draft board. Draft administrator General Lewis B. Hershey ordered them drafted immediately. Indignant Congressmen raised an embarrassing question: if military service was the honorable duty the government said it was, how could General Hershey use it as a punishment?

A new Resistance battle cry began to be heard: "Make love—not war!" Instead of going to jail, many draft resisters decided to seek political refuge in Canada. Sympathetic Canadians organized a Committee to Aid American War Objectors, which found shelter and jobs for the exiles. Some in the Resistance disapproved, considering flight a "cop-out" from the antiwar struggle. But in a speech at Toronto, Resistance lawyer William Kunstler declared, "I would hope, myself, that every American of draft age came across the border here or

went to Sweden; then they wouldn't have to fight any-
body's wars."

Draftees in uniform began to resist. In 1966 three
refused to board ship for Vietnam, insisting that the new
Army Field Manual prohibited them from obeying illegal
orders. A court-martial sent them to military prison for
three years.

President Johnson persisted in escalating the war because public opinion polls in 1966 showed that even after
New York Times reporters in North Vietnam revealed
that American bombs were killing noncombatant women
and children and destroying schools and homes, a large
majority of Americans still favored intensifying the
bombing. Antiwar demonstrations were disapproved by
sixty-two percent who, deaf to the message of the
Resistance, considered protesters draft-dodgers or Communists.

"The man who offers the American masses any kind of
benefit will have their support for any type of foreign
policy," wryly observed former Dominican President Juan
Bosch, "because the masses haven't the least idea of
anything outside of their fear of Communism and their
hunger for advantages."

M.I.T. Professor Noam Chomsky agreed. "Consciousness has yet to create mass resistance . . . . The
cities of North America remain smug and complacent—
with the significant and honorable exception of the
student youth."

In 1967 Army doctor Howard Levy was court-martialed
for refusing to train U.S. Green Berets as medical aid men
for Vietnam. Accusing the Green Berets of being "liars
and thieves and killers of peasants and murderers of
women and children," he introduced proof at his trial that
they tortured prisoners and paid bounties to Montagnard
tribesmen for the ears of Viet Cong they killed. He was
sent to prison for three years.

Draft card burner Don Baty publicized his resistance by
seeking sanctuary in a Methodist church. Reverend Finley

Schaef refused to turn him over to U.S. marshals, insisting, "He has committed no crime in refusing by conscience to kill." The marshals climbed over the bodies of a hundred nonresistant sympathizers protecting Baty at the altar. Seized, handcuffed and carried out, he raised two fingers defiantly in the V peace sign.

"Why was I handcuffed?" he asked later. "Were the U.S. marshals afraid I would love somebody while they weren't looking?" Fasting in jail, he refused to accept a lawyer and would not walk to the courtroom handcuffed. "I am not simply a number to be handcuffed, ordered around, tried and sent off to a penitentiary. I am Donald Baty, a young human being, struggling to cope with a bewildering world."

He was sentenced to four years in prison.

In the spring of 1967, over 200,000 New Yorkers staged an antiwar demonstration during which 175 youths carrying signs urging, "Burn Draft Cards, Not People," set the example. Congress turned a deaf ear in June by renewing the draft, without change or reform, after only fifteen minutes of debate.

"Nothing can undo the pettiness of Congress," observed the *New York Times*, "in yielding to the ugly spirit of some of its least enlightened members." SDS reacted with an angry call for an escalation of strategy "from protest to resistance." A Committee of Draft Resistance was formed in July by SDS, university professors, Quakers and clergy. Joan Baez, a founder, urged all Americans to "organize and encourage resistance to, disruption of, and noncooperation with all the warmaking machinery of the United States."

In September 320 scientists, writers, professors and ministers, including Nobel Prize winner Linus Pauling and Bishop James A. Pike, pledged to raise funds for the movement.

The next month, the Resistance organized a march on the Pentagon that brought 55,000 people to Washington. The Administration nervously put 20,000 armed forces on standby alert at nearby military bases. The mass of demonstrators were nonviolent, but a handful of militants charged the Pentagon's front entrance, scuffling with MP's and marshals.

"This was the turning point," said Jerry Rubin. "It's the end of mere picketing and the beginning of disruption."

Dr. Benjamin Spock, the famous baby specialist, told a crowd at the Lincoln Memorial, "The enemy, we believe in all sincerity, is Lyndon Johnson, who was elected as a peace candidate in 1964 and who betrayed us within three months."

The new militant mood was evident throughout October in antiwar civil disobedience erupting all over the country and on university campuses. In Oakland, two thousand demonstrators sat down in front of the induction center to block entry. They returned day after day, despite daily arrests of twenty-five to a hundred people, including Joan Baez. "We simply don't have enough courts," admitted the district attorney of Alameda County, "so we have to take the most militant leaders."

When ten thousand demonstrators finally surrounded the induction center, building barricades and blocking the streets, two thousand police were called in from thirteen cities. The crowds refused to disperse. Forming a flying wedge, helmeted police smashed into them, clubbing and Macing newsmen along with demonstrators. California Governor Ronald Reagan called their action "in the finest tradition of California law-enforcement agencies."

One imprisoned draft resister bitterly told Dr. Willard Gaylin, "I think our government is too insensitive to respond to anything except violence and destruction . . . . How else do you deal with a structure that has no conscience?"

Yale Chaplain William Sloane Coffin, Jr., Dr. Spock and three other noted members of the Resistance defied the draft law by encouraging Boston youths to burn their cards. "We hereby publicly counsel these young men, to continue in their refusal to serve in the armed forces."

declared Coffin, "as long as the war in Vietnam continues, and we pledge ourselves to aid and abet them in all the ways we can. This means that if they are now arrested for failing to comply with a law that violates their consciences, we, too, must be arrested, for in the sight of that law we are now as guilty as they."

When they were arrested, Coffin wrote, "While no one has the right to break the law, every man upon occasion has the duty to do so. This was just such an occasion, and my own conclusion is that the war is so unjust as to justify attempts to organize massive civil disobedience . . . . When laws begin to dominate rather than to serve men, far from staving off chaos, they begin to invite it . . . . Not to serve the State has upon occasion appeared the best way to love one's neighbor . . . . Many Americans whom we now hail as heroes were in their generation notorious lawbreakers . . . . Washington, Hamilton and Jefferson were traitors all until success crowned their efforts and they became great patriots."

Spock and Coffin were convicted by a Federal court in Boston, but their convictions were reversed on appeal. The judge agreed with the defendants that "vigorous criticism of the draft and of the Vietnam war is . . . protected by the First Amendment, even though its effect is to interfere with the war effort."

Senator Eugene McCarthy grew convinced that the truth about the Vietnam War was beginning to get through to the American people, and he made it the central issue of his challenge to the President for the Democratic nomination in 1968. He scored an astonishing political upset in the New Hampshire primary race, encouraging Senator Robert Kennedy also to try to win the nomination. Dismayed, Johnson withdrew as a candidate for renomination, rather than risk humiliation by being repudiated by his own party.

Some within the Resistance began using violent tactics. One group bombed the New York draft office, another the draft board in Lancaster, Pennsylvania. Boards in

Berkeley and Madison were firebombed, and a fire was set inside the National Headquarters of Selective Service in Washington, D.C.

In May, 1968, two priests, the brothers Philip and Daniel Berrigan, led seven other Catholic dissenters in breaking into the draft office at Catonsville, Maryland. They burned 600 draft files with napalm, then gave themselves up for arrest.

Father Dan Berrigan had visited Hanoi, where he had shared a bomb shelter with Vietnamese children during U.S. air raids. Returning home, he had visited the deathbed of a Syracuse, New York, high school boy who had set himself afire in despair over the war. "I knew I must speak and act against death," he declared, "because this boy's death was being multiplied a thousand fold in the Land of Burning Children. So I went to Catonsville and burned some papers because the burning of children is inhuman and unbearable."

Defense lawyer William Kunstler told the jury, "They were trying to make an outcry, an anguished outcry to reach the American community before it was too late. I think this is an element of free speech to try, when all else fails."

The Berrigans were found guilty and sentenced to three and a half years in prison. Father Dan jumped bail to continue his resistance in the underground. Over three-hundred people risked jail to shelter him as he moved from one family to another, meeting with peace groups. It took four months for the FBI to apprehend him. Soon afterward, his brother Philip and six other dissenters were indicted for plotting in prison to kidnap Presidential adviser Henry A. Kissinger, to force an end to the Vietnam War and the freeing of U.S. political prisoners.

Their defense was headed by former Attorney General Ramsey Clark, by that time a vigorous antiwar critic. He exposed the government's star witness, Boyd F. Douglas, Jr., as a convicted forger and confidence man used by the FBI as an agent provocateur to discredit the anti-war movement. Douglas was forced to admit he had been paid $9,000 by the FBI. The jury was deadlocked ten-to-two in favor of acquittal, and a mistrial was declared. Conspiracy charges were later dropped against the Harrisburg Seven, but Phil Berrigan had two years added to his sentence for smuggling letters out of prison to peace groups.

The climax of the Resistance came in Chicago in August, 1968, with huge, dramatic antiwar demonstrations outside the Democratic Convention. The Johnson forces that controlled the convention were determined to nominate Vice President Hubert Humphrey. Mayor Richard Daley of Chicago cooperated by harassing the ten thousand antiwar demonstrators who flocked into the city. Refusing to allow peace marches, he ordered his police to rough up the Resistance.

"Few of the protesters wanted violence," noted Ramsey Clark. "Time and again they sought real communication, real negotiation, intermediaries. But the city had a different policy—no negotiation, no tolerance for troublemakers . . . . Law enforcement did not follow the law . . . . We saw the grim possibility of a police state . . . . [Demonstrators experienced] a raw demonstration of police capacity for violence, and they will never forget it."

Television cameras recorded this brutality for a shocked nation. On the floor of the Convention, Senator Abraham Ribicoff denounced "Gestapo tactics in the streets of Chicago." Of three hundred newsmen assigned to cover the event, sixty-three were beaten, had their equipment smashed, or were arrested for filming what a Presidential commission later described as a "police riot." Over five hundred indignant delegates and clergymen led a candlelight march of protest through the streets of Chicago.

The Johnson forces had rigged the Convention against Eugene McCarthy and were able to nominate Hubert Humphrey. But their use of brutal force against the Resistance shattered the unity of the Democratic party.

Bitter over Chicago, millions of Democrats abandoned the party and assured the election of Republican Richard Nixon, who promised to end the war.

Johnson wrote later, "Fighting between police and students . . . in Chicago proved to every television viewer in America how deep the cleavage was in our society, how intense the hatreds." He accused the Resistance of prolonging the war by encouraging the North Vietnamese and Viet Cong.

But historian Arthur Schlesinger, Jr., replied, "If Ho Chi Minh *thinks* the American people are divided, one reason surely may be . . . that they *are* divided . . . . Our adversaries are fighting not because they expect us to collapse but because they believe fanatically in their own cause . . . . Our bombing has hardened the resolve of North Vietnam a good deal more than anything said by Martin Luther King."

Antiwar pressure began to make itself felt within the military. In October 1968 a sit-down strike was staged by twenty-seven prisoners in the Army stockade at Presidio, California, over brutal treatment. The youths, whose average age was nineteen, were given average sentences of fifteen years each for "mutiny." Public outrage, stirred by the Resistance, compelled the Judge Advocate General, in an unprecedented action, to cut down the sentences to two years each. The uproar also forced the Army to drop court-martial charges against eight GIs at Fort Jackson arrested for engaging in antiwar activities.

Secretary of the Army Stanley Resor hastily issued a directive to all commanding officers, "Guidance on Dissent," warning them "to impose only such minimum restraints as are necessary to enable the Army to perform its mission." The Army also began granting an increasing number of applications by GI's demanding discharge as conscientious objectors.

A third annual mobilization of Clergy and Laymen Concerned About Vietnam convened in Washington in February 1969. The Reverend William Sloan Coffin, Mrs.

Coretta King and other antiwar leaders met with Kissinger, who assured them that Nixon intended to "wind down the war" as quickly as possible. But the war continued throughout the whole four years of Nixon's first term. As he gradually withdrew troops, he expanded bombing raids.

In June a group of Philadelphia Quakers attempted to read a list of Americans killed in Vietnam from the steps of the Capitol. Each time they tried, they were arrested, photographed, fingerprinted and charged with unlawful assembly; some were jailed. After Senator Jacob Javits denounced this persecution, a General Sessions judge ruled that the Quakers' act of war resistance was peaceable and nondisruptive.

On Moratorium Day, October 15, 1969, over 300,000 peaceful demonstrators, the largest crowd in American history, marched on Washington. Vice President Spiro Agnew had predicted that demonstrations would "dry up and disappear" under a Nixon Administration. But endless crowds poured past the White House in a forty-hour vigil called the March Against Death. Signs with the names of dead American soldiers and destroyed Vietnam villages were carried along a four-mile route.

Nixon angrily let it be known that he would not look out the window but would watch a football game on TV instead. When the huge crowds joined folk singer Pete Seeger in singing, "Give Peace A Chance," Dr. Spock called out, "Are you listening, Nixon?"

Watching from the Justice Department, Attorney General John Mitchell, later involved in the Watergate scandal, muttered to his wife, Martha, "It looks like the Russian Revolution!"

Worried by the Moratorium, the President ordered Secretary of Defense Melvin Laird to stop all "search and destroy" missions in Vietnam; announced the "resignation" of unpopular draft director General Hershey; and appealed to the "great silent majority" of Americans to support his program. Through Vice

President Agnew, he put pressure on the television networks to censor the broadcast of news programs showing the brutality of the American war effort in Vietnam.

A sensational new trial began in September 1969 when the Chicago Eight—Jerry Rubin, Abby Hoffman, Dave Dellinger, Rennie Davis, Tom Hayden, John Froines, Bobby Seale and Lee Weiner—were charged with conspiracy to cause a riot at the Chicago Democratic Convention. Nixon was determined to use the trial to brand the Resistance as a radical plot.

The case was tried before Judge Julius Hoffman, who grew infuriated at the defendants for their disrespect and mockery of the proceedings. Abby Hoffman set the tone for the trial by declaring, "I should plead guilty by reason of sanity." Telling the district attorney, "I've never been on trial for my thoughts before," he blew kisses at the jury.

Judge Hoffman, a totally humorless man, snapped, "The jury is directed to disregard the kiss thrown by the defendant Hoffman." He termed the proceedings "just another criminal trial," but the defendants quickly proved it to be a political confrontation between the Resistance and the government.

On Moratorium Day the defendants wore black armbands to court to memorialize the dead in Vietnam. Before court opened, Dave Dellinger rose to read off the names of G.I.s killed in action.

Defendant Bobby Seale refused to stand trial until the lawyer of his choice recovered from an illness. When Judge Hoffman admonished him to be silent, he snapped, "I admonish you. You are the one in contempt of people's constitutional rights." For calling the judge a "fascist, racist pig," he was ordered bound, gagged and shackled to a chair.

Continuing to protest by rattling his chains, he inspired defense counsel William Kunstler to cry out, "Your Honor, when are we going to stop this medieval

torture? . . . . I feel so utterly ashamed to be an
American lawyer at this time!"

When Seale was unbound and ungagged, he refused to
stop protesting. Judge Hoffman then separated him from
the trial and sentenced him to four years in jail for contempt, a harsh sentence without precedence in recent
history.

As the government sought to prove conspiracy charges
against the Chicago Eight (now reduced to the Chicago
Seven), Jerry Rubin mocked the proceedings by wearing
an orange sweatshirt bearing the word "Conspiracy." He
told the press, "This is the greatest honor of my life. I hope
that I am worthy of this great indictment, the Academy
Award of Protest."

In his testimony, Abby Hoffman explained the Yippies'
theory of resistance: "The institutions of America were
crumbling . . . . All we had to do was sit there, smile and
laugh, and the whole thing would come tumbling down because it was basically corrupt and brutal."

The District Attorney argued, "They would have us
believe that their revolution is in a lofty cause, and so they
can break the laws to achieve it . . . . When a protest becomes a violent, deliberate and forcible assault on public
order, it can never be excused or tolerated . . . . These
men have named St. Matthew and Jesus . . . Lincoln and
Martin Luther King. Can you imagine those men supporting these men?"

"Yes, I can!" shouted Dellinger's daughter from the
spectators' benches. "I can imagine it because it is true!"

While the jury deliberated its verdict, Judge Hoffman
took reprisals against the defendants and their lawyers by
reading off a list of their "contemptuous acts" and sentencing them to jail terms of up to four years for contempt.

"This is a travesty on justice," Dellinger protested, "and
if you had any sense at all you would know that the record
that you just read condemns you and not us."

Spectators cried, "Tyrants! Tyrants!" Marshals dragged
them from the courtroom.

Rennie Davis declared, "Judge, you represent all that is old, ugly, bigoted and repressive in this country."

Kunstler said, "We are being punished for what we believe in."

Abby Hoffman warned, "When the law is tyranny, the only order is insurrection."

Jerry Rubin promised, "By punishing us you are going to have ten million more."

The jury acquitted all defendants of the charge of conspiracy. But in a compromise, five were found guilty of individually seeking to promote a riot. One juror later explained, "Those of us who disagreed were urged to go along so that the whole conduct of the trial could be tested on appeal."

Before being sentenced, Abby Hoffman told the court, "[The D.A.] says we are un-American. I don't feel un-American. I feel very American . . . . It is not that Yippies hate America. It is that they feel the American dream has been betrayed." Judge Hoffman sentenced each to the maximum term of five years in jail and a five-thousand-dollar fine. He denied bail.

Rennie Davis said, "My jury will be in the streets tomorrow all across this country."

Tom Hayden declared, "We were chosen by the government to serve as scapegoats for all that they wanted to prevent happening in the 1970s."

Abby Hoffman said, "If Lincoln had given his first inaugural speech in [Chicago's] Lincoln Park, he would be on trial right here."

Jerry Rubin told Judge Hoffman, "Julius, you have radicalized more young people than we ever could."

Protest demonstrations against the trial broke out in Washington, Boston, Chicago and other cities. Yale historian Staunton Lynd declared, "The government says the defendants conspired to riot. I, on the contrary, say that they organized a process of petitioning just as Sam Adams and Tom Jefferson did before them."

An appeals court overturned Judge Hoffman's denial of bail, and the defendants were released from jail. A Federal appeals court also later overturned all his contempt sentences and set aside his sentences on the charges because of his own obviously prejudiced conduct on the bench.

American bar associations were deeply upset by the trial of the Chicago Seven, feeling that political trials did not belong in the criminal courts. They also deplored prosecution under an antiriot law of doubtful constitutionality, because it restricted the free movement of political dissenters about the country. The Resistance cited the trial as proof that the government sought to suppress protest and free speech.

Meanwhile the number of draft resisters and Army deserters grew steadily. In 1969 alone the Army admitted to over 73,000 desertions. Draft resister cases began to pile up at the rate of three hundred a month, jamming the courts.

The country was stunned in January 1970 when a suppressed story about atrocities committed at My Lai and other Vietnamese villages by American troops was exposed by veterans who had been there. Public sentiment finally began to swing in favor of the Resistance when it was revealed that U.S. troops had fired point blank into huddled groups of elderly men, women, children and babies, murdering 567 of them.

"The gradual shift of Vietnam sentiment from hawk to dove, first in the Senate and then more grudgingly in the House," observed *New York Times* correspondent Warren Weaver, Jr., "was heavily influenced by constituent mail."

Mayor John Lindsay of New York told two thousand Philadelphia college students that he had "unending admiration" for those who refused to serve in Vietnam and were willing to take the consequences: "These are the guys who are heroic." Referring to the trial of the Chicago Seven, he said, "After that dubious exercise, a disaster for all concerned, it is harder to believe that the system is open, fair-minded and humane."

Popular resistance intensified in May, 1970, when President Nixon expanded the war into Cambodia. The campuses erupted in fresh protest demonstrations, and the Senate threatened to cut off military funds. In an attempt to force the Supreme Court to rule the Vietnam War illegal, the Massachusetts legislature passed a bill upholding the right to resist being drafted for an undeclared war.

Over 200,000 orderly war protesters staged a new March for Peace in Washington. Acting under Administration orders, police made mass arrests of seven thousand on the first day, and almost six thousand subsequently—a record high for arrests in any civil demonstration in American history. The prisoners were penned in temporary detention centers. The vast majority were released without charges being filed because the arrests were illegal.

In San Francisco a crowd of 156,000, the largest West Coast demonstration ever, launched a simultaneous protest.

New vindication for the Resistance came in June, 1971, when Daniel Ellsberg turned over the classified Pentagon Papers to the *New York Times*, which defied the Nixon Administration's attempt to prevent their publication. The Papers exposed much of what the government had told the American people about the Vietnam War as lies and misrepresentation.

Professor Roger Fisher of Harvard observed, "The *Times* and its officers . . . engaged in a form of civil disobedience."

Resistance persisted all through 1972. In June a group of two hundred professional people including Dr. Spock, Yale psychiatrist Robert Jay Lifton, actress Candace Bergen and producer Joseph Papp, staged a sitdown in the Senate hallway to petition for an end of the war. Senator Edward Kennedy told them, "We must keep this issue on the front burner. It is the number one issue in this country." Police arrested 111 protesters.

Early in 1973, the long, exhausting efforts of the Resistance finally compelled President Nixon to forego seeking military victory in Vietnam and accept truce terms similar to those that had been offered by Hanoi four years earlier. The President called the truce "peace with honor," insisting that it had only been made possible by his four years of escalating the war into Laos and Cambodia, conducting huge bombing raids on Hanoi, and mining the harbor of Haiphong.

"One thing is fairly clear," wrote James Reston in the *New York Times*. "There has been a sharp decline in respect for authority in the United States as a result of the war."

President Nixon could not forgive the Resistance for the role it played in opposing his continuation of the war throughout his first term. Once the American ground role in the war had ended, he refused to consider amnesty for the thousands of draft resisters who had sought political asylum in Canada, France and Sweden. Every previous President in American history, as well as most nations in the world, had granted such amnesty at the conclusion of every war.

12 The Student Resistance

During the 1950s, college students in America were considered "the silent generation." Intent upon winning their diplomas, getting a good job and joining the Establishment, most discreetly kept silent while Senator Joseph McCarthy led a repressive movement against free speech and thought.

But early in the 1960s a small, determined resistance movement developed among radicalized middle-class students. Alienated by America's materialistic society, they rebelled against the pursuit of success, money and possessions. Wearing torn blue jeans and beards, they sought to "do their own thing" as individuals, seeking personal values instead of conforming to the expectations of corporations and parents.

They organized as the Students for a Democratic Society (SDS) at Ann Arbor, Michigan, in June 1962. Tom Hayden, twenty-two, wrote their declaration of independence, the Port Huron Statement, which asserted that life in the United States was frustrating, that the system was rigid and obsolete, that society's leaders mouthed hypocritical platitudes, and that job opportunities were both overrated and corrupting to youth.

SDS called for mass resistance to make the American government and economy more responsive to human needs. Condemning the Cold War as a bankrupt foreign policy, SDS vowed to work nonviolently for a "New Left," using the campus as a fulcrum to promote resistance and change.

A handful at first, the youthful founders of SDS soon had active chapters operating in college after college. Their first campaign was against the "multiversity"—huge state universities like Berkeley, which had an enrollment of over thirty thousand, where education was an impersonal, assembly-line affair, where mostly graduate students taught, while many professors spent their time in war-related research for the Pentagon.

SDS students at Berkeley led a protest against the refusal of administrators to give either students or faculty a voice in making university policy. They demanded the right to be treated as adults and dealt with as equals. The Dean of Students replied in September, 1964, by banning their activities in front of the campus gate. Student organizations joined SDS in a defiant "united front" picket line. Eight student leaders were punished by suspension.

When police tried to arrest a student speaker, three thousand students surrounded the police car and refused to let it leave. Philosophy student Mario Savio sprang to its roof and held a "Free Speech" rally that lasted for two days. SDS then led sit-in protests in various university buildings.

When police were summoned to clear them out, the students went limp and had to be carried to detention centers. Indignant at the arrests, the student body, supported by many faculty members, called a general strike that brought the university to a virtual standstill.

Paraphrasing Thoreau, Savio told students, "There is a time when the operation of the machine becomes so odious, makes you so sick at heart, that you can't take part . . . and you've got to put your bodies upon the levers . . . and you've got to make it stop. And you've got to indicate . . . that unless you're free, the machine will be prevented from working at all."

SDS's Free Speech Movement compelled University of California president Clark Kerr to offer new and liberal rules for student protest, and to promise that none of the eight hundred sit-down demonstrators would receive university punishment. Savio and the more radical students demanded greater concessions to student power, but the strike ended when the Berkeley faculty and the moderate student majority accepted Kerr's concessions.

The winds of change swept from Berkeley through the campuses of America. Students everywhere began organizing and demonstrating, under SDS leadership, for four principle demands—university reform, equal rights for blacks, a priority for human values over financial concerns, and getting out of Vietnam.

Most demonstrations were nonviolent where the college administration resisted panic and showed a willingness to negotiate on reasonable demands. Campus disorders occurred chiefly when police and the National Guard were called in against the demonstrators and employed violence.

"The beating of students who occupied university buildings in protest against injustices," observed Dr. Spock, "has intensified the processes of alienation and radicalization because it has revealed the academic authorities, in calling on the police for violence, as morally no better than the police in this respect and as snugly in the same Establishment bed with government, Pentagon, and industry."

In 1965 the student Resistance held campus "teach-ins" to disseminate suppressed truths about the Vietnam War. The hawkish Senate Internal Security Subcommittee issued a report trying to smear the student antiwar movement as Communist.

Students staged demonstrations against the invasion of campuses by recruiters from the military, the CIA and corporations aiding the war effort, especially Dow Chemical, manufacturers of napalm. University of Penn-

sylvania students exposed their university for conducting germ war research for the Pentagon.

"The protesters feel that the hypocrisy of industry in
supplying napalm in the name of peace-seeking," observed University of Toledo sociologist Joseph W. Scott,
"is exceeded only by that of the universities in their
willingness to provide military manpower to carry on the
war."

Students demanded an end to the draft, protesting its
unfairness to poor blacks and Puerto Ricans who could not
afford to go to college and therefore could not claim a
student exemption. Instead of ending the draft, the
Johnson Administration struck back at graduate students,
many of whom were leaders of the Resistance, by ending
their exemption.

"To young men who asked nothing but to be left alone to
pursue their own lives," observed Professor Charles A.
Reich in *The Greening of America*, "the State brought the
peremptory demand that they join the armed forces, subject themselves to a coercive discipline, training, and in-
doctrination, and then take part in a mass killing of the
people of another race, for purposes they did not believe
in . . . . If someone destroys a person's world, and he finally begins to resist, does that make him the aggressor?"

Johnson's decision to begin bombing North Vietnam led
some radical students to escalate the Resistance by
bombing targets at home. The Weatherman faction of SDS
went underground to blow up ROTC buildings on campus
and set fire to military research laboratories. They
operated at night to avoid killing anyone, but a number of
people were injured.

Meanwhile student unrest was spreading around the
world, one example inspiring another, much as frustrated
students had touched off a chain of worldwide revolts in
1848. The French paper *Le Monde* carried over two-thou-
sand stories on student resistance on six continents during
the school year 1967-1968.

In France, stormy student demonstrations—the May Movement of 1968—were led by Daniel Cohn-Bendit. Protesting intolerable overcrowding of the Sorbonne and a repressive examination system, they were set upon by police who entered the Sorbonne hurling tear gas grenades. Thousands of angry students poured out of classes to throw up street barricades.

After days of fighting, 948 students had been arrested, and almost 700 students and police had been injured. French Educational Minister Alain Peyrefitte shut down the Sorbonne. Young workers angered by police brutality toward strikers joined forces with the student Resistance. Their combined demonstrations shook the government of Charles de Gaulle and compelled him to reorganize the whole university system.

Students in Italy, West Germany and other nations also took to the streets to demand similar reforms.

In the United States that spring, a new resistance movement was sparked by SDS at Columbia University, where students were incensed by an authoritarian administration. Indoor antiwar demonstrations had been banned with the explanation that "The administration will not tolerate efforts to make the university an instrument of opposition to the established order."

When militant Mark Rudd became president of SDS in March 1968, he won a vote to raise student resistance to the level of confrontation. The issue chosen was the decision of Columbia to build a gym on parkland used by poor blacks whose neighborhood surrounded the university.

When eight hundred protesting students seized and barricaded five university buildings for five days, President Grayson Kirk called a thousand policemen on campus to drive them out. Over seven hundred were arrested and so roughly handled that 150 students and faculty were injured. Outrage led five thousand students and faculty to respond to SDS's call for a mass strike.

Kirk was compelled to cancel classes and exams for the remainder of the school year. The strikers held their own "teach-ins." In a second police action that injured sixty-eight more resisters, two hundred more students were arrested. The university suspended seventy-five students as ringleaders and flatly refused SDS demands for a student voice in administration policy.

The administration's use of police force polarized the campus, radicalizing many students who at first had disapproved of SDS's confrontation tactics. Dr. Kirk complained, "Our young people, in disturbing numbers, appear to reject all forms of authority . . . and they have taken refuge in a turbulent and inchoate nihilism whose sole objectives are disruptive."

He was answered by Harold Taylor, former president of Sarah Lawrence College, who said, "If the university and its present leadership fails to act, either to stop the war, reform the archaic curriculum, grant legitimate student rights, take its students seriously, take a stand against racism and racial injustice, what else can serious people do, students or anyone else, than move beyond acquiescence into protest and resistance?"

The Columbia student strike eventually won some of its demands, and Dr. Kirk was compelled to resign. The Columbia example was quickly copied on other campuses.

When the president of San Francisco College sought to discuss the grievances of student resisters, he was fired on orders from Governor Ronald Reagan. Over two thousand students staged a protest demonstration. Acting president S. I. Hayakawa called in San Francisco's Tactical Squad, which attacked and dispersed the rally, beating up spectators in the process. An infuriated student body and faculty went on strike, forcing Hayakawa to shut down the college.

By June, 1969, a Harris Poll showed students in revolt on two out of three American campuses. Another poll revealed that prior to the use of police against students, ninety percent of students had held a favorable opinion of police, whereas now ninety percent considered them brutal and unfair.

At the University of Michigan, students horrified the community of Ann Arbor by announcing that they were going to napalm a dog. When indignant citizens protested, the students asked them, "Why are you so upset about our proposal to napalm a dog, when you support your government in napalming thousands of women and children in Vietnam every day?"

Such selective morality also led Vice President Agnew to ignore what the Resistance was protesting, while branding the resisters as " 'vultures' . . . and 'parasites' [whom] we can afford to separate . . . from our society with no more regret than we should feel over discarding rotten apples from a barrel."

At the end of 1967 Robert Kennedy painted a dramatic picture of an American society tearing itself apart: "Demonstrators shout down government officials and the government drafts protesters. Anarchists threaten to burn the country down, and some have begun to try—while tanks have patrolled American streets and machine guns have fired at American children . . . .

"Half a million of our finest young men struggle, and many die, in a war halfway around the world; while millions more of our best youth neither understand the war nor respect its purposes, and some repudiate the very institutions of a government they do not believe."

Studies in 1968 showed that the student Resistance had become a mass movement to be reckoned with. It had even reached down into sixty percent of all high and junior high schools, according to one survey by the National Association of Secondary School Principals. The Urban Research Corporation found over 215,000 students active in demonstrations, almost 3,700 with arrest records. Three out of four demonstrations were wholly peaceful, and during 1968 they had succeeded in winning thirty-one percent of student demands.

"Student protests have in great degree been motivated by extraordinary selflessness, idealism and altruism," observed the ACLU in April 1969. When students demonstrated to demand job opportunities for blacks in the construction of Buffalo campus buildings, Governor Nelson D. Rockefeller declared, "I think that students have assumed a share of social responsibility in the life of our community, and I applaud them for it."

At Berkeley, students joined with hippies, Yippies and other "street people" in May, 1969, to turn a dusty three-acre plot owned by the University of California into a "people's park." They raised $1,000, planted trees, and installed benches, a children's sandbox and swings. Their intent was to demonstrate the possibilities of "people power" in action, against the bureaucratic control of public property.

Chancellor Roger Heyns sent police and bulldozers in at dawn to destroy the park and guard the ruin with National Guardsmen. The president of the Berkeley student body led a march of eighteen hundred dissenters to take the park back. A three-hour battle ensued with police, who fired shotguns loaded with birdshot. Over sixty people went to the hospital; one died.

During three days of clashes, 2,200 National Guardsmen were called out, along with a helicopter that sprayed searing CS tear gas over residents of the whole area. There were 900 more arrests and 150 more injuries. Over 170 outraged faculty members boycotted classes in protest. The university erected an eight-foot fence around the disputed three acres, surrounding it with Guardsmen to prevent the reopening of the People's Park.

Newsweek published a photograph showing three girl students sitting on the ground facing rows of gasmask-wearing Guardsmen with uplifted rifles and fixed bayonets. The editors asked, "When youthful citizens can be wantonly gassed and beaten, all because of a small, unauthorized park, what has happened to America? What has happened to our sense of perspective, our tradition of tolerance, our view of armed force as a last—never a first—resort?"

The extension of the Vietnam War into Laos and Cambodia by the Nixon Administration in 1969 unleashed a new wave of student demonstrations. Most were peaceful until the police were called in. At Ohio State University police threw tear gas cannisters, and students threw back rocks and bottles.

Disorders grew worse when twelve hundred National Guardsmen with fixed bayonets were rushed to the campus. Over five-hundred demonstrators were arrested; sixty students and thirty-five police were injured. Order was restored only when the police and Guardsmen were withdrawn. Then student and faculty marshals moved among the enraged crowds of students urging them to "cool it."

At Princeton the student body and faculty went on strike proclaiming that "the strike will continue until Princeton takes an institutional stand against the war and severs all ties with the Department of Defense." The Stanford faculty condemned the President's commitment of American troops to Cambodia as "unwise, immoral and hostile." The National Student Association urged Nixon's impeachment. Over half of the demonstrations occurred at schools that had not previously had any.

When National Guardsmen were brought on campus at Kent State in Ohio, they hurled tear gas at demonstrating students, then opened fire. Four uninvolved students, two boys and two girls, were killed. These deaths, witnessed by horrified millions on television newscasts, provoked the first sustained national strike in the history of American higher education. Over 450 colleges and universities shut down in protest. Some enraged students set fire to ROTC buildings, while others inflicted damage on other military property on campus.

Ten days after the Kent State killings, black student demonstrators at Jackson State College in Mississippi were attacked by police. Two were killed and ten wounded.

When the Gallup Poll asked Americans to name the country's biggest problem in 1971, the trouble most often cited was the seething unrest on college campuses.

Writer Samuel Grafton, in an interview for *Lithopinion*, asked famed Swedish sociologist Gunnar Myrdal what he thought had stirred students to such passionate resistance.

"The war in Vietnam is fundamental to the radicalization of youth everywhere," Myrdal replied. "It has started young people everywhere thinking about causes and events."

Admitting himself a little shocked by the excesses of both sides in campus clashes, he added, "At the same time I am disturbed because many of the demands of the students are quite sensible and I find myself wondering why the administrators didn't think of those things for themselves . . . . Why shouldn't there be democratic organizations of students?"

Sweden had escaped serious unrest, he explained, by treating its students as adults with the right to participate in faculty meetings and university decisions.

In an interview with Theodore White, President Nixon blamed permissive parents for the rebellion against authority by students: "They were given too much too easily, and this weakened them." If the life style of most students was not approved by the White House, it was clear from the turmoil on campus that they in turn did not approve of the President.

When the Resistance finally forced an end to American involvement in the Vietnam War, the campuses fell relatively quiet once more. Although many student demands remained unsatisfied, many university administrations had been compelled to give student councils a voice in university policy; to give up military contracts with the Pentagon; to eliminate or decredit the ROTC; to make the curriculum more meaningful; to open up admissions to more minority students; to liberalize university regulations; and to refrain from calling police or the National Guard on campus to suppress student demonstrations.

These were no small gains for a minority group that, prior to the Sixties, had been totally powerless.

13 Black Power
Flexes Its Muscles

Black resistance in the United States received a tremendous impetus in May, 1954, with the Supreme Court decision in *Brown v. Board of Education of Topeka* that "separate but equal" schools for blacks were unconstitutional. Encouraged to resist all other forms of discrimination, blacks began demanding equality in employment, housing and the use of public facilities.

Senator James Eastland of Mississippi urged defiance of the Supreme Court decision and its implications. White Mississippian business and professional men organized a White Citizens Council (WCC), which quickly spread through the South. The movement was aimed at "keeping the Nigra in his place," by the use of economic pressure, legal obstruction, intimidation and arrests. Although the WCC did not itself practice physical violence, it encouraged violence on the part of workingclass Southern whites in the Ku Klux Klan.

Fear kept many Southern blacks from bringing lawsuits to enforce the Supreme Court decision. Northern blacks and sympathetic whites came south as "freedom riders" to organize them into resistance groups to demand their civil rights, including the right to vote.

In 1955, when Mrs. Rosa Parks was arrested for refusing to sit in the back of the bus in Montgomery, Alabama, the

Reverend Martin Luther King led the Southern Christian Leadership Conference (SCLC) in an eleven-week boycott of that city's busses. He and 115 followers were arrested, but their indictments were overturned in December, 1956, when the Supreme Court agreed with them that bus segregation was illegal. Yet when blacks then sought to integrate the busses, twenty-two more were arrested. Not until 1959 were such arrests declared illegal by the Court.

Blacks were learning that it was not enough to have Federal law on your side, even a Supreme Court decision, if the power of local law enforcement was against you. Many realized that they could win their civil rights only to the extent that they were willing to put their bodies on the line in open resistance, risking beatings, vituperation, arrests and loss of jobs.

The black Resistance needed more college-trained young people to lead that struggle. In 1956 the NAACP sought to compel segregated Southern colleges to admit black students. A Federal Court order forced the University of Alabama to admit 26-year-old Autherine Lucy, but the presence of a black girl on campus provoked rioting by half the student body, augmented by outside mobs. The university forced her withdrawal.

Charging that the university had conspired to force her out, she won a Federal Court order directing her reinstatement. Two days later, trustees expelled her for making "outrageous, false and baseless accusations" against the university.

At Little Rock, Arkansas, backed by a Federal Court order, a group of black students sought to enter Central High School for the fall, 1957, term. State troops barred their entrance on orders from Governor Orval Faubus. A white mob chased away a fifteen-year-old black girl, screaming, "Lynch her!" A subsequent attempt to enroll was also thwarted by a white mob of a thousand.

Denouncing the "disgraceful occurrences" at Little Rock, President Dwight D. Eisenhower ordered Federal troops to prevent mob rule and enforce the law. Nine black pupils were escorted to class under the protection of fixed bayonets.

Protesting that Arkansas had been placed under "military occupation," Governor Faubus accused the soldiers of "bludgeoning innocent bystanders, with bayonets in the back of [white] schoolgirls and the warm, red blood of American citizens staining the cold, naked, unsheathed knives."

Six years after the Supreme Court had ordered all school boards to end segregated education "with all deliberate speed," only four percent of the South's black students had succeeded in winning admission to white schools. And in many of the integrated schools, white parents had withdrawn their children and sent them to hastily organized all-white private schools.

To compel the South to respect civil rights, several hundred middle-class black college students organized the Student Nonviolent Coordinating Committee (SNCC) in 1960. Julian Bond described early meetings of the executive committee in Southern cities: "The exchanges would go something like this: 'I was arrested four times in the last thirty days, how about you? . . . . Well, I haven't been arrested, but I've been beaten up twice.' "

SNCC's first important campaign of civil disobedience took place in Greensboro, North Carolina, when four black college freshmen ordered coffee at a "white only" Woolworth lunch counter. Refused service, they remained quietly seated until the store closed. The next day they returned with sixteen more undergraduates who demanded service. By the end of the week, hundreds of students were sitting in at both Woolworth's and the S. H. Kress store.

The civil rights movement shifted into high gear as SNCC spread sit-ins to a hundred southern cities, involving fifty thousand nonviolent demonstrations. Arrests soared into the thousands, accompanied by police brutality.

SNCC next concentrated on voter registration drives, hoping to build black power at the polls, especially in rural Southern communities where blacks outnumbered whites. James Farmer's Congress of Racial Equality (CORE) helped SNCC break the chains of fear that kept blacks out of voting booths.

In 1961, when thirteen CORE freedom riders, six whites and seven blacks, took the bus south for New Orleans, the bus was fire-bombed in Alabama, and the demonstrators were beaten with chains and brass knuckles. Freedom rider James Peck wrote, "The thing you must remember to do when you get involved in one of these things is always to remain nonviolent. Another thing you should remember is to protect your head and face with your hands. I remembered the first . . . but I guess I just didn't do too good a job of covering up . . . . They put fifty stitches in my head and face to put me back together again."

A riot of serious proportions occurred in 1962 when Governor Ross Barnett vowed to prevent the integration of the University of Mississippi by "standing in the doorway" to bar an attempt to enroll by black student James Meredith. Retired general Edwin Walker, a Right-wing extremist, called for ten thousand volunteers to rally at Oxford to support Barnett.

When Meredith was escorted on campus by a small force of Federal marshals, an inflamed white mob of segregationist students and outsiders attacked them in a fifteen-hour battle. The riot was quelled by three thousand troops, but not before two journalists were killed and seventy people wounded. Troops were forced to remain in Oxford for over a year to protect Meredith.

Although many impatient blacks were now advocating matching violence with violence, Martin Luther King urged black people not to lose faith in the eventual redemption of the white man and in the power of nonviolent civil disobedience.

Supported by SNCC and CORE, he launched a massive civil rights campaign in the spring of 1963. In Birmingham,

Safety Commissioner Eugene (Bull) Connor used savage police dogs to attack black men, women and children as they marched and sang "We Shall Overcome." They were also knocked down by powerful streams of water from fire hoses so deadly that they ripped bark off trees and tore bricks out of walls.

March leaders urged King's followers to remain nonviolent. One shouted through a bullhorn, "We want to redeem the souls of people like Bull Connor." Almost twenty-five hundred demonstrators were arrested and jailed.

In August, King organized a March on Washington, one of the largest peaceful demonstrations in the nation's history. Its climax was his famous speech, "I Have A Dream," delivered at the Lincoln Memorial before a mixed audience of 200,000 supporters.

"I have a dream that one day on the red hills of Georgia the sons of former slaves and the sons of former slaveowners will be able to sit down together at the table of brotherhood," he cried eloquently. "I have a dream that even the State of Mississippi, a state sweltering with people's injustices, with the heat of oppression, will be transformed into an oasis of freedom and justice. I have a dream that my four little children will one day live in a nation where they will be judged not by the color of their skin but by the content of their character."

In 1964 President Lyndon B. Johnson, succeeding the assassinated John F. Kennedy, persuaded Congress to pass the Civil Rights Act of 1964. Banning discrimination in the use of all public facilities, it compelled and assisted school desegregation, promised equal job opportunities, and guaranteed black voting rights. But once again, blacks found that the law on paper was not necessarily the law in practice.

The black Resistance raised the cry for "Freedom Now!"—not when reluctant states decided to get around to obeying Federal law. Massive protests began in the North as well as the South against inequities of job opportunities, education and housing. Northern discrimination was more subtle, operating behind realtors' refusal to rent apartments or sell houses to blacks outside ghetto areas.

As black impatience increased because expectations aroused by Supreme Court decisions and acts of Congress were frustrated on the local level, crime and violence increased in the ghettos. Police harassment intensified black wrath.

In July, 1964, when a fifteen-year-old black youth was shot to death in Harlem by an off-duty white police lieutenant, that ghetto erupted in a riot. Jesse Gray, leader of a Harlem rent strike against slumlords, appealed to a furious crowd for "a hundred dedicated men who are ready to die for Negro equality."

Disturbances began with the funeral of the dead boy; bottles were hurled at police from rooftops. The police responded with gunfire. Before the night was over, fifteen people had been shot, one fatally, and 116 injured, including a dozen policemen. Black moderate leader Bayard Rustin was booed and shouted down as an "Uncle Tom" when he sought to calm the crowd.

"I'm prepared to be a Tom," he replied, "if it's the only way I can save women and children from being shot down in the street, and if you're not willing to do the same, you're fools." But the crowds were out of hand. Mobs roamed the Harlem streets, looting stores, attacking whites and jeering at police. Violence continued for several days. It touched off other large-scale rioting in Brooklyn and Rochester, New York.

Black militants raised the cry "Power to the people!" They demanded community self-government for the ghettos. The Johnson Administration took a step in that direction by setting up the Office of Economic Opportunity (OEO), with an appropriation of almost a billion dollars for a "war on poverty." The OEO was administered locally by black leaders.

In the summer of 1964 SNCC and CORE organized a Mississippi Summer Project to set up "freedom schools," register black voters, and share the physical danger that was part of every black person's life in Mississippi. About eight hundred white college students joined the freedom riders heading south.

Angry Mississippi segregationists destroyed almost forty black churches and beat up hundreds of summer workers, many of whom were arrested and jailed. Three—two whites and a black—were found murdered and buried at the base of a dam.

The following summer, the King credo of nonviolent civil disobedience suffered a severe setback in the black ghetto of Watts, a Los Angeles district seething with discontent over high unemployment, bad housing and police badgering.

"Negroes who had never expected decency or fair play from the police of Mississippi," noted Algernon D. Black, former Chairman of the New York Civilian Complaint Review Board, "had hoped for something better in California . . . . But the police harassed and hounded them. Stopping cars driven by Negroes, searches, rough talk, over-ready guns, insults, humiliations—for months these were daily occurrences in an increasingly tense atmosphere of insensitivity to human feelings."

The trouble began with the arrest of a young black for speeding. When a sullen crowd gathered, tempers flared. Police struck one bystander and roughly handled a young black woman. A riot erupted, escalating swiftly until ten thousand blacks were involved. Smashing, looting and firebombing white-owned businesses, they did thirty-five million dollars worth of damages. National Guardsmen opened fire on the rioters. Thirty-four people were killed, over a thousand were injured, and almost four thousand were arrested.

One of the worst civil disorders in American history, Watts marked a sharp break with the nonviolent leadership of Martin Luther King. Black youths told investigators, "These _____ cops have been pushin' me 'round all my life. Whitey ain't no good. He talked 'bout law and order; it's his law and his order; it ain't mine." . . . . "If I've got to die, I ain't dyin' in Vietnam; I'm going to die here." . . . . "The white man got everything. I ain't got nothin'." . . . . "Whitey use his cops to keep us here. We are like hogs in a pen—then they come in with those silly helmets, sticks and guns . . . ."

Advocates of Black Power urged more explosions like Watts to stun the nation into paying attention to black grievances. But the nonviolent black Resistance argued that riots were self-defeating. Almost two years after the Watts rebellion, little had changed in that ghetto. The buildings that had been burned down had not been rebuilt. Worse, many store proprietors had been frightened away, making life harder for area residents.

Watts, however, marked a significant change in black thinking. Many blacks became less interested in integration than in seeking racial solidarity through their own institutions, communities and culture. Young militants calling themselves Black Panthers raised the slogan "Black is beautiful!" to develop racial pride and erase the stigma attached to blackness from slave days. Rejection of the white culture was emphasized by Afro hair styles, dashikis, Black Power handshakes and the celebration of black heroes of history.

SNCC's chairman, Stokely Carmichael, became the spokesman of the Black Power movement. "We have to wage a psychological battle for the right of black people to define their own terms, define themselves as they see fit and organize themselves as they see fit," he declared in a speech at Berkeley in November, 1966, adding, "We are tired of trying to explain to white people that we're not going to hurt them. We are concerned with getting the things we want, the things that we have to have to be able to function . . . . Will white people overcome their racism and allow for that to happen in this country?"

A more militant black mood was evident in a 1966 "Black Power March" in Mississippi. Most of the marchers were from Mississippi itself. Attacked by a white mob armed with hoes and axe handles, they fought back with their fists.

"We are not going to stay ignorant and backward and scared," declared Annie Devine of the Mississippi Freedom Democratic Party.

Floyd McKissick, national director of CORE, agreed, "I'm committed to nonviolence, but I say what we need is to get us some black power."

Ghetto riots blazed in Newark and Detroit during the hot summer of 1967, with 162 other ghetto clashes—and eighty-three deaths—by September. The President's National Advisory Commission on Civil Disorders put the primary blame on police racism and repression. Bayard Rustin cited another cause.

"The Vietnam war is also partly responsible for the growing disillusion with nonviolence among Negroes," he declared. "The ghetto Negro does not in general ask whether the United States is right or wrong to be in Southeast Asia. He does, however, wonder why he is exhorted to nonviolence when the United States has been waging a fantastically brutal war, and it puzzles him to be told that he must turn the other cheek in our own South while we must fight for freedom in South Vietnam."

Nothing shocked and enraged American blacks like the assassination of Martin Luther King in March, 1968, at Memphis, where he had gone to lead a march of black sanitation workers for decent wages. His killer was an escaped white convict, James Earl Ray, who kept silent about his motive when arrested. Blacks were convinced that he had been hired to murder King by fanatical Southern segregationists.

Black wrath exploded across the nation. Racial rioting erupted in 125 cities, with buildings going up in flames, wild looting, attacks on police and firemen, and gun battles in the streets. Crowds gathered in the ghettos to listen

to furious speakers denounce white America. In
Washington, D.C., at least seventy fires were set and
police made over four thousand arrests. A machine gun
was set up on the steps of the Capitol, and troops guarded
the White House.

The nation was stunned and dismayed. Millions of
whites as well as blacks grieved for the death of Dr. King.

"We must move from resistance to aggression," cried
Black Panther H. Rap Brown, "from revolt to revolution!"

Resorting to armed resistance, the Panthers clashed
with police in city after city. Although the Justice Department denied it, police raids on Panther headquarters
to seize stockpiles of weapons seemed synchronized to
wipe out the Panthers as a force. Many Panthers were shot
and killed.

A split developed in Panther ranks between leaders
who considered violent tactics suicidal and those who felt
that only armed resistance could protect the ghettos.

Meanwhile the black Resistance continued operating at
the campus level. In 1969 alone, black student protests at
eighty-five universities forced increases in black admissions, and the introduction of black studies. At UCLA
over two thousand students and faculty held a protest
rally when black instructor Angela Davis was fired for her
Marxist views.

"The path of liberation," she told the crowd, "is marked
by resistance at every crossroad; mental resistance,
physical resistance . . . . Learn from the experience of
the slave."

A 1969 survey of blacks in Newark found sixty-three
percent convinced that blacks could win their goals
without violence, while fifty-two percent felt that King's
nonviolent strategy was losing its hold on black people. In
the next year Newark elected its first black mayor,
following the example of Cleveland and Gary.

Angela Davis and Bobby Seale both went on trial in 1970
for crimes of violence. When both were acquitted, the

nonviolent black Resistance cited these victories as proof that blacks should not despair of white American justice.

But by 1972 most white Americans had been antagonized by ghetto riots, crime in the streets and enforced bussing to segregate the schools. They overwhelmingly reelected Richard M. Nixon, regarded by the black community as unsympathetic to black aspirations. Black leaders determined to work within the system, electing more blacks to public office.

A new day dawned in the Black Power movement when Bobby Seale, cofounder and chairman of the Black Panthers, ran for Mayor in Oakland as a Democrat in April, 1973, and came in second. Their ranks depleted by police raids and disputes among the leadership, the Panthers had switched from bullets to ballots. Instead of black berets and battle fatigue dress, they now wore suits and ties and campaigned peacefully.

Bayard Rustin observed, "Stokely Carmichael lives in Africa—he has dismissed America as unreconstructably racist . . . . H. Rap Brown is in jail. Eldridge Cleaver is in exile under house arrest in Algeria . . . . They failed to recognize that the overwhelming majority of blacks oppose violence: what took place in Watts and Newark only reinforced the conviction that devastation and bloodshed produced by urban insurrection visits itself most severely on blacks."

After the stormy clashes of the Sixties, most blacks agreed that the nonviolent civil disobedience of Martin Luther King had been the right way in the first place.

14 Other American Resistance Movements

One of the most significant resistance movements in the United States during the Sixties was the revolt of youth against adult society. Determined on a life style of their own, they firmly resisted the clothing, hair styles, shaving, social drinking, moral codes, conventions, conformism, racial prejudice, economic goals and Sunday Christianity of their elders. They waged, in effect, a nonviolent cultural revolution.

"If adults admired their long hair more, the young would probably cut it off themselves," wryly observed social critic Marya Mannes. "The only thing apparently intolerable to them is our approval, for then what are they revolting against?"

Young blue collar workers also resisted as spurious goals the older generation's advice to work hard at boring jobs, to be loyal to the corporation, and to strive for suburban status and security. A small number of young students and workers dropped out of the "rat race" to join communes in the country or city, farming or turning out arts and crafts.

The Yippies resisted American values by opting for a more joyful, spontaneous life style. They demonstrated scorn for the Establishment's reverence of money by visiting the gallery of the New York Stock Exchange to shower brokers on the floor with dollar bills during peak trading hours.

"It simply blew their minds," reported Abby Hoffman, grinning.

Environment-minded youth resisted the flagrant pollution of our air and water by American industries. Their campaign won so much public support that legislators quickly took up the cry, even against corporations that had contributed to their campaign funds. The government got into the act in 1970 by sponsoring an "Earth Day" celebration that let young people work off steam. Millions participated across the nation as half the Nixon cabinet made antipollution speeches. But no effective government funds accompanied the lip service.

"The Earth Day affair," observed Washington correspondent I. F. Stone, "was a gigantic snow job . . . . [The President] turned in a budget which allocates fifty-two cents of every general revenue dollar to the military and space but only four-tenths of one cent per dollar to air and water pollution."

Resistance to educational discrimination came from minority groups who protested that their children were being denied a quality education by white educators unsympathetic to minority needs. They demanded community control of schools.

Mexican-American students in California found it difficult to relate to an education that taught only an Anglo view of American history, ignoring their Mexican heritage and banning the Spanish language used by their parents at home. In March, 1968, they organized "blowouts"— walkouts in East Los Angeles schools. Over five thousand striking students presented school authorities with a list of forty grievances. Some demonstrators were arrested, but many of the strike's demands were won.

"The students today have the guts our parents didn't," declared one Brown Beret leader. "The Mexican

American has just discovered how the democratic process works, after years of watching on the sidelines."

In New York City black and Puerto Rican groups called a strike against white control of ghetto schools. There was some violence when white teachers insisted on crossing their picket lines. The President angrily told aide Frank Shakespeare, "When they hit the teachers over the head . . . they have no right to run the school."

Counter-resistance developed among white groups in the inner city who opposed what they perceived as a threat to their community by blacks. In Brooklyn they opposed the admission of thirty-two black and Puerto Rican children transferred to Canarsie schools, fearing the move as a precursor of integrated housing that would turn Canarsie into a slum. Their boycott closed down six elementary and two junior high schools.

"The thing about what happened here," declared Father Genarro Simoneti, "is that there is right on both sides. On the one hand, the black people have a right to have their children educated. On the other hand, the white people have a right to preserve their community."

"We're not trying to move in with them," replied Joan Boatright, a black mother. " . . . It's just quality education that we're after."

Resistance stiffened on both sides of the issue, not only in New York but throughout the country. In many communities whites organized demonstrations against the bussing of black students to white schools and white students to black schools. Their demand for "neighborhood schools" was countered by blacks who pointed out that large numbers of rural white students already rode busses to central schools without complaint.

White demonstrators resorted to violent methods to resist court orders compelling bussing. In 1971, ten empty school busses were blown up in Pontiac, Michigan, eight days before 8,700 children were supposed to be bussed to integrated schools. In March, 1972, President Nixon proposed legislation to deny courts the power to order bussing to achieve racial integration. He advocated instead more Federal aid to ghetto schools. The following year he slashed all Federal educational funds.

The Reverend Theodore M. Hesburgh, chairman of the U.S. Civil Rights Commission, criticized the President's program as a step backward in the cause of equal rights.

Resistance groups also formed on both sides of the issue of religion in the schools. When school boards ordered daily prayers in public schools, opposed parents resisted all the way up to the Supreme Court, which upheld their contention that this practice violated the separation of church and state required by the Constitution. Prayer-minded parents angrily resisted this ruling by backing legislation to authorize "voluntary" school prayers but failed to win its passage.

A massive taxpayers' Resistance developed during the Sixties as the cost of living soared, along with local, state and Federal taxes. Congress was flooded with angry protests demanding that tax loopholes be closed for rich individuals and corporations. President Nixon responded by slashing the national budget, except for $81 billion in military appropriations. Refusing to spend funds for bills voted by the Congress, he warned Americans that to do so would cost them a fifteen percent increase in taxes. In many communities school budgets were voted down to prevent increases in property taxes.

To resist the nation's treatment of the poor, Dr. Ralph Abernathy, successor to Dr. King, led a Poor People's March to Washington. The demonstrators built a shantytown—"Resurrection City"—in front of the Lincoln Memorial, camping there for two months. Millions of TV viewers heard their grievances on newscasts.

"Few who watched failed to learn," noted Ramsey Clark. "The poor people . . . spoke of hunger in America, of welfare robbing people of their dignity, of racism and schools that failed to teach. They reminded us that the law spoke of equal justice, while they had no rights."

President Nixon responded by proposing a guaranteed annual wage for all but did not press the plan when it bogged down in Congress over the question of how much the country could afford to guarantee every family.

In various parts of the country, rent strikes were used to resist landlords who charged exorbitant rents while denying tenants essential services. Tenant unions withheld rent checks, depositing them instead with the state attorney general until the landlords agreed to meet tenants' demands.

Striking tenants in New York City's Harlem ghetto had despaired of getting the city to do anything about the lack of running water and heat in slum tenements, not to mention rat attacks on sleeping children. Strike leader Jesse Gray took reporters on a tour to show them atrocious conditions, violations of the building code "overlooked" by city inspectors.

"This is the worst thing I've seen in all my years of reporting," angrily declared Homer Bigart, Pulitzer-Prize-winning reporter of the *New York Times*. When New York papers ran front-page stories on the rent strike, Mayor Robert Wagner was forced to send a bill to Albany legalizing the rent strike until slumlords made their properties livable.

Another important resistance movement of the Sixties was Women's Liberation. "No organized group protest—and in a decade that has produced so many—came so quickly, so powerfully. . .to impose itself on the American scene," observed editor Midge Decter, "as did the women's liberation movement. Within something like two years of its first official stirrings, women's lib swept to the top of . . . the American cultural mood."

Women's Lib became a prime topic for TV talk shows and magazine and newspaper articles. Members invaded and integrated male-only bars and clubs. Some invaded the *Ladies Home Journal's* editorial offices and won the right to edit a whole issue from their viewpoint.

Women's Lib not only successfully changed the society's patronizing stereotypes of the female role but also won equal rights for many women. The telephone company was forced to pay several million dollars to women to make up for higher wages paid to men for the same work. Police departments, fire companies, military academies and other heretofore all-male precincts were forced to accept female applicants. Congress passed an Equal Rights Amendment for women, although many state legislatures balked at ratifying it as a constitutional right.

One of Women's Lib's greatest successes was its campaign to abolish anti-abortion laws. Whether a woman chose to terminate a pregnancy or not, Women's Lib insisted, was a private matter between her and her physician, not something for male legislators to decide. The Supreme Court agreed. A counter-resistance was mounted by a Right to Life movement, which tried to have the states continue to outlaw abortions.

Resistance to deteriorating mail service grew after the Nixon Administration removed the Post Office from the government and put it in private hands to "modernize" it. Letters sent by airmail on a one-hour flight arrived five days later. One disgusted citizen in upstate New York delivered his own letter by cycling from one town to another, proving that this beat the U.S. mail by several days. Congress was flooded with so many protests that Postal Service head Elmer T. Klassen was forced to go on TV with promises of swift improvement.

A citizens' Resistance with 200,000 members, Common Cause, was headed by former Health Education and Welfare Department Secretary John W. Gardner. Its purpose: To "return the government to the people." Common Cause stopped big corporations with defense contracts from paying off helpful politicians by big campaign contributions. It exposed how much money candidates were collecting, and where it came from. It also joined with Consumers Union in class action lawsuits against big corporations to end abuses of the consumer.

Consumer resistance was spearheaded by Ralph Nader, the incorruptible crusader who organized a band of idealistic young lawyers and investigators to expose shoddy production and overpricing by American corporations. Thanks to Nader, car owners were no longer at the mercy of Detroit's big auto companies. The young lawyer's exposes, which commanded respect in Congressional hearings, forced Detroit to recall millions of already-sold cars to correct dangerous defects.

"Consumers have begun to make themselves heard in legislative hearings, before regulatory agencies, and in the courts," observed Philip J. Dodge, an official of the Cooperative League of the USA. "They have gained a grudging respect from lawmakers . . . who earlier had hardly recognized their existence, and from business itself."

Upset by rising food prices in March 1973, a Michigan woman protested by mailing 388 small peanut butter sandwiches to the White House. When the news media picked up the story, groups of women around the country banded together in FIT (Fight Inflation Together), organizing a week's boycott of meat to resist enormous price jumps.

President Nixon at first declared himself opposed to all price controls on food, and Secretary of Agriculture Earl Butz called anyone who wanted them "a damfool." A few days later, when it became apparent that the meat boycott was winning nationwide support, the President hastily changed his mind and imposed price controls on meat. Secretary Butz then declared that he hadn't really meant the "damfool" remark.

But women did not consider it a victory to have a price freeze imposed on meat at the highest prices in history, prices most families could not afford. They went ahead with their boycott anyway, demanding a twenty percent rollback of prices. The boycott cut meat sales by twenty-five percent and brought down prices in some areas, although not permanently. FIT promised to continue its resistance to high food prices indefinitely.

For decades, large-scale agriculture in the Southwest had been dependent on Mexican-American or native Mexican workers who were poorly paid, badly housed and fed, and ill-educated. In September, 1965, at Delano, California, Cesar Chavez organized grape workers who went on strike—"La Huelga"—against the state's giant corporate farming enterprises. Despite threats of assassination, Chavez kept the strike going.

"It was four years ago that we threw down our plowshares and pruning hooks," he declared in 1969. "These Biblical symbols of peace and tranquility to us represent too many lifetimes of unprotesting submission to a degrading social system that allows us no dignity, no comfort, no peace. We mean to have our peace, and to win it without violence."

To dramatize his resistance, he went on a hunger strike. In further imitation of Gandhi, he called for a national boycott of grapes. His nonviolent struggle won widespread sympathy and support, and in 1970 many growers were compelled to sign union contracts guaranteeing a two-dollar minimum wage.

When Chavez sought to organize farm workers in Arizona in 1972, the Arizona legislature hastily passed a law to prohibit farmworkers from striking, picketing and boycotting. Chavez promptly called for massive civil disobedience of a law which was clearly unconstitutional.

Indians, too, were resisting injustices of long standing. In December, 1969, one group of young Indians sailed across San Francisco Bay in the middle of the night to occupy Alcatrez Island, abandoned as a federal prison. Painting "Indian Land" on one building, they invited other Indians to join them.

A thousand Indian men, women and children took up quarters in the empty cell blocks. They maintained that under an old Sioux treaty, they had the right to any unused Federal land. They saw nothing ironic in seeking a prison as a prize.

"The reservation is also a prison," shrugged Sid Mills, a 21-year-old Yakima from Washington.

Student leader Denis Turner declared, "We're just asking for some of the things stolen from us so we can govern ourselves."

Dennis Hastings of the Omaha tribe said, "My folks back home on the reservation are proud of us and what we're doing. If we have to, we'll fight for this island. They can kill us but they can't kill our spirit." The Indians held out for about a month but were finally evacuated from the island peacefully by government forces.

In February 1973, two hundred members of the American Indian Movement (AIM) seized the South Dakota prairie hamlet of Wounded Knee, where the U.S. Cavalry had once slaughtered three hundred Sioux men, women and children. To dramatize their dissatisfaction with the Indian Bureau's treatment of Indians, they proclaimed their secession from the United States.

Over three hundred FBI agents and Federal marshalls surrounded Wounded Knee, attempting by turns to coax, threaten or starve the Indians into submission. Senator Edward Kennedy called for a full-scale Senate investigation of government treatment of Indians. Senator J. William Fulbright asked for an investigation of 371 Indian treaties broken by the government.

In late March, 1973, millions watched on TV as Marlon Brando was given an Academy Award as the best actor of the year. As an act of resistance in support of the Indians at Wounded Knee, he refused the award through Apache Princess Sacheen Littlefeather, citing Hollywood's derogatory portrayals of Indians. His gesture caused the Screen Actors Guild to meet with film producers and agree that future films would be fairer, creating "a new image for the Indian."

Meanwhile AIM leader Russell Means declared, "The government has two choices. Either they attack and wipe us out like they did in 1890, or they negotiate our reasonable demands."

The Indians held out at Wounded Knee for over two months until the government finally agreed to negotiations.

15 Tactics and Frustrations

The less responsive a government is to protest, the more violent resistance is likely to become. "If ever the free institutions of America are destroyed," wrote Alexis de Tocqueville in *Democracy in America* in 1834, "that event may be attributed to the omnipotence of the majority, which may at some future time urge the minorities to desperation and oblige them to have recourse to physical force. Anarchy will then be the result, but it will have been brought about by despotism."

After World War II, the world was swept by revolutionary movements against colonial and dictatorial governments that refused to permit peaceful change. The United States, itself a country born of violent revolution, supported the repressive governments in the name of stopping Communism.

In the process, it became increasingly deaf to the voices of the Resistance at home. One black antiwar militant asked, "What business have I got fighting for 'freedom' halfway around the world when I don't have any on my own street?"

If the Vietnam War polarized the nation, it also split the Resistance over the question of tactics. Militants insisted that only violence would compel the media and the government to pay attention and make the American people aware of the violence inflicted in their name on people in Vietnam.

But the followers of Gandhi disagreed. "Nonviolence requires more militancy than violence," declared Cesar Chavez. "Nonviolence forces you to abandon the shortcut in trying to make a change in the social order. Violence, the shortcut, is the trap people fall into when they begin to feel that is the only way to attain their goal."

Violent or nonviolent, the tactics that seemed most effective were those that were sustained. A 1969 Urban Research Corporation survey showed that only twenty percent of one-day student protests induced a college administration to negotiate grievances. Half of all protests lasting at least two days, however, won negotiations. So did seventy percent of strikes and building seizures lasting over a week.

For two years before the seizure of buildings at Columbia University for a student sit-in strike, the administration had turned a deaf ear to SDS demands that it end participation in the Vietnam war effort. SDS had begun by using only mild resistance tactics—exposing secret war research in Columbia labs; placing "war crimes" posters at recruiting sites; staging "guerrilla theater" antiwar skits; holding forums and rallies. Ignored, SDS had escalated tactics to blocking the entrances of administrative offices and recruiting sites.

The next stage in escalation involved tipping over recruiting tables and removing military and defense industry recruiters physically from campus. Only when the administration still refused to negotiate antiwar grievances did SDS disrupt the university by seizing and holding buildings.

The longer the government persisted in prolonging the Vietnam War, the more difficult it became for moderate leaders of the Resistance to keep protest nonviolent. They were forced themselves to employ tactics of "direct action"—destroying draft board records. Antiwar extremists began blowing up banks, government buildings and the headquarters of defense industries. Unfortunately for the Resistance, violent and nonviolent groups were often confused in the public mind.

The tactics of the nonviolent Resistance were designed to force news coverage by the media. Government spokesmen could air their views at length to thirty-five million people at a time on TV, and to another fifty million readers of newspapers and magazines. Students mounting soapboxes to appeal to a hundred or two hundred people through a bullhorn could not possibly hope to compete in the national marketplace of ideas.

Hence the Resistance sought headlines by acts of civil disobedience—draft-card burning, sit-ins, obstruction tactics, unauthorized demonstrations. When dissidents were arrested, the American Civil Liberties Union (ACLU) defended their tactics as a form of free speech to balance the grossly unfair opportunies of the Establishment. Such tactics also served to stir the apathetic majority into paying attention to acts of injustice.

"Winning supporters usually has to be done by dramatic or ingenious methods," noted Dr. Spock, "because most people, though basically committed to justice, will try to ignore injustice as long as possible, to avoid the multiple pains of involvement."

Those in the Resistance must do more than just talk about change; they must *make* things change. By organizing demonstrations, they invite sympathizers to join their ranks and become part of the struggle. They compel others sitting safely on the fence to get off it and choose sides.

The nonviolent Resistance has a wide choice of tactics in addition to those named above—strikes, boycotts, fasts, teach-ins, preach-ins, underground newspapers, petitions, pledges of resistance, marches, and refusal to obey a protested law in front of newsmen. Some consider raids on draft boards to be nonviolent acts of civil disobedience.

In Indianapolis the "Beaver 55" group not only made

such raids but also invaded Dow Chemical laboratories to destroy records used in napalm and nerve gas research.

"Some of the draft boards in Indianapolis haven't been able to draft men because of the files which were destroyed," Jo Ann Mulert said in May, 1970. "The records at the Dow offices were very important for their continued war research. Also, we wanted to do something dramatic enough to get other people involved, to make them think about the issues and commit themselves to doing something about them."

Her fellow raider Tom Trost added, "We wanted people to realize that human life is more important than property, that property should be destroyed if necessary to save lives."

Asked why they had turned themselves in, Jo Ann Mulert explained, "We had to surface in order to make it clear to people what we were doing. We had to counteract the media and the people who wanted to brush us off . . . [as] vandals."

Satire can be an effective Resistance tactic, notes Yale Law Professor Charles A. Reich. At Community College of New York, antiwar students laughed Reserve Officers Training Corps drills off campus by matching them with slapstick imitations. Berkeley students disrupted bureaucratic paper-shufflers in administrative offices by staging a "mill-in," surging in and out to present all kinds of absurd documents.

Yippies Abbie Hoffman and Jerry Rubin won headlines with their satirical tactics. To mock the Democratic Convention in 1968, they chose a pig as the Yippie candidate. They showed reporters a spray they called their answer to Mace—it caused police to "develop love feelings toward demonstrators." They also gravely announced a plan to "levitate" the Pentagon off its foundation, destroying its gravity and power.

Serious symbolic acts can be an equally effective form of resistance. When the Berrigans invaded draft offices to pour blood on the files, no explanations were necessary.

The ACLU, committed to the defense of all peaceful, nonobstructive forms of protest, does not, nevertheless, hold that noble ends justify the use of ignoble means. It also warns that unfair tactics alienate the press and public opinion.

In December 1968 New York University students prevented an address by a Saigon official by draping him in a Nazi flag, drenching him with water and pelting him with an egg. When former UN Ambassador Arthur Goldberg tried to address a conference, he was shouted down by thirty students who dumped the head of a pig on the speaker's table.

Dr. Spock observed, "When demonstrators invade an audience that has gathered to hear a certain speaker and by their uproar keep him from being heard, the audience is infuriated and so is the neutral public that reads about the episode in the news." He called upon the Resistance to eschew counterproductive tactics—forcibly disrupting classes, throwing rocks and stink bombs, jostling school administrators, taunting police and carrying signs with offensive language.

Those who seek change in the system succeed best when their demonstrations are calm, dignified and persuasive. Millions of Americans watching the Chicago National Convention in 1968 on TV were shocked by the speech, appearance, signs and behavior of some antiwar demonstrators. Instead of being appalled at the savage brutality of the police in attacking demonstrators, many felt that they had "asked for it." A handful of young radicals had, in fact, sparked the police riot by taunts.

"The activists have correctly gauged the temper of the police," notes historian Richard Hofstadter in *American Violence*," who are often quite ready to oblige by lashing out indiscriminately against both those who have offended them and . . . orderly demonstrators, innocent bystanders, reporters, cameramen. Young radicals have thus found a way to put the police and the mass media to work for them, as the public sees a hideous spectacle of beating, kicking and clubbing by officers of the law against unarmed demonstrators and witnesses."

Those who demanded that the Resistance turn violent had their strongest argument in the attempt of the Nixon Administration to smother anti-war protests. In November, 1969, when 300,000 demonstrators marched past the White House, the President pressured all three TV networks to deny them live coverage, while he himself watched a football game on TV instead.

Federal Communications Commissioner Nicholas Johnson warned that by "bottling up legitimate means for communication of dissent" the Administration would "leave only the avenues of violence and despair."

Republican Senator Jacob Javits noted that "an insidious form of repression" of dissent was being "tolerated, if not actually condoned, at the highest level of our Government."

The Resistance was discouraged when one survey on the Vietnam War showed that of those who had come around to agreeing that it had been a mistake, sixty percent were also against the anti-war demonstrators. Most Americans were upset by the small number of those who used violent anti-war tactics but not upset by the government's use of violence in Vietnam or at home. A Gallup Poll survey showed that fifty-eight percent of the public blamed demonstrating students, not the National Guard, for the killing of four students at Kent State by Guardsmen. The government had skillfully managed to persuade most Americans that the issue of the day was "law and order" rather than justice, which is what the Resistance was all about.

Despite that fact, it had been the peaceful civil disobedience of the majority in the Resistance that had improved civil rights, made changes in the university system, forced Lyndon Johnson out of the White House, made peace a major issue in the 1968 election campaign, and turned most Americans against the war.

On the other hand, the Resistance had failed to keep the Nixon Administration from dragging on the war for four more years, from expanding it into Laos and Cambodia, from mass-bombing North Vietnam and mining its harbors, from increasing the military budget and cutting down on social services, and from failing to enforce civil rights laws effectively.

Some in the Resistance felt that its tactics had not been forceful enough. "Appealing to people's moral conscience will get you almost nowhere," complained Brown University graduate Ira Magaziner in his commencement speech, "and it's very frustrating . . . . The mass of American people are apathetic and commit the sin of inaction on most issues . . . . The only way to wake up people who are asleep is to jar them awake and disrupt their sleep rather than trying to whisper to them while they snore."

Many dissenters, discouraged by the failure to "turn America around," simply dropped out of the Resistance and turned their backs on the Establishment. Some joined communes looking for a "brotherhood of love." Some, beaten and jailed too often, gave up the social struggle for justice to seek meaningful change instead in their own personal lives.

"Goliath is too powerful," said one dejected David.

16 "Law and Order"

Goliath was not above using dirty tricks in seeking to suppress and discredit the opposition, as a dismayed American people discovered in 1973, with the exposure of the shocking Watergate scandal that compromised the Nixon Administration.

In some cases agents provocateur were used to infiltrate Resistance groups. These government spies not only compiled dossiers on leaders and members but also often supplied weapons and bombs, urging violent tactics so that the Justice Department could arrest and imprison Resistance leaders.

The government also sought to cripple the Resistance by passing restrictive laws. Under the Anti-Riot Act passed in 1968, it became possible for the Administration to punish anyone for traveling around the country and aiding the Resistance, or even for making an anti-Establishment speech. The Act was used to persecute the Chicago Seven, other antiwar groups, and militant black civil rights leaders.

"The college student who helps black Mississippi sharecroppers to organize," pointed out the ACLU, "may be found to have had an intent to 'aid and abet' one of them in carrying on a riot . . . . 'Outside agitators' may stop 'agitating' in the places where 'agitation' would be most significant and where, if things are ever to change, it is most needed."

In April, 1971, President Nixon sought to break up a week of peaceful anti-war demonstrations in Washington by ordering five thousand police backed by twelve thousand troops to make mass arrests of close to thirteen thousand people. Almost seven thousand were jailed on the first day alone, an all-time record. With inadequate detention facilities, hundreds were held in a football field. Because almost all the arrests were made illegally, charges against all but a few were dropped, once the government had succeeded in hampering the demonstrations.

"A dangerous precedent has been established," warned a *Nation* editorial. "On another tomorrow, the numbers arrested may be even larger, their detention longer . . . . What the Administration did, as the ACLU correctly points out, was to sacrifice law in the 'interest of order'— that is, its conception of order. Actually, the dragnet arrests were a breakthrough in the direction of . . . lawlessness."

Many of those caught up in the mass arrests sued the government for damages, especially those who were simply innocent bystanders watching the demonstrations. The first two suits to reach court in October, 1972, were decided by a Federal district judge against the government. Two Federal employees were awarded damages of $4,500 each.

The Justice Department illegally wiretapped the phones of members of the Resistance. When FBI agents attempted to intimidate SDS by investigating its members, Dean Idzdrda of Wesleyan University refused to cooperate. "It's unfortunate that a climate of suspicion can be created by such activity that might lead some students to be more circumspect than the situation requires," he declared. "Things like this can be a danger to a free and open community, if men changed their behavior because of it."

In December, 1970, Senator Sam Ervin, the Senate watchdog on constitutional rights, was shocked to discover that the Army had snooped on over eight hundred civilians in Illinois, including Democratic Senator Adlai E. Stevenson III, civil rights leader the Reverend Jesse Jackson, and Democratic Congressman Abner Mikva, prominent opponents of the Vietnam War.

The Administration did not hesitate to reward open violence against Resistance demonstrations. In May, 1970, when students marched in New York City to protest the Kent State killings, they were attacked by a crowd of a thousand construction workers. Police turned their backs while the hard-hats beat up the students. President Nixon summoned their union leader, Peter Brennan, to the White House and told him, "I want you and all members of the building and construction trades to know how pleased I was to see the tremendous outburst of support for our country." Brennan was later appointed Secretary of Labor for the Nixon Administration.

Before the American Civil Liberties Union put a stop to it, many students in the Resistance were illegally deprived of their student deferments in the draft. Those who refused to be inducted were sent to jail or forced into exile. Any serviceman who dared voice criticism of the Vietnam War faced a court-martial.

Long before Vietnam or Watergate, the government had often used its powers to suppress criticism by liberals and radicals. In the fifties they had been subpoenaed by the House Un-American Activities Committee (HUAC), whose inquisitional proceedings sought to brand them as "un-American" and blacklist them from employment, or jail them for "contempt of Congress."

Yet in the Supreme Court decision of *West Virginia v. Barnet*, Justice Robert H. Jackson had written, "If there is one fixed star in our Constitutional constellation, it is that no official, high or petty, can prescribe what shall be orthodox in politics, nationalism, religion or other matters of opinion or force citizens to confess . . . their faith therein."

HUAC's most celebrated victims were leading film writers, actors and directors who resisted the Committee's headline-hunting attempts to probe their political beliefs.

In 1947, when HUAC sought to compel actor Lionel Stander to name "subversives" he knew, he replied scathingly, "I know of a group of fanatics who are desperately trying to undermine the Constitution of the United States by depriving artists and others of life, liberty and the pursuit of happiness without due process of law . . . . This Committee."

Resisting HUAC's interrogation, writer Albert Maltz declared, "I would rather die than be a shabby American groveling before [HUAC committeemen] . . . who now carry out activities . . . like those carried out in Germany by Goebbels and Himmler."

HUAC secured contempt of Congress citations against writers known as the Hollywood Ten, who were promptly discharged by their film studios, blacklisted by the Motion Picture Association of America, and sent to jail. They later sued the film producers for conspiracy to blacklist them; four major studios settled out of court for a sum over $107,000.

Albert Einstein had been denounced by anti-Semitic HUAC chairman John Rankin of Mississippi as a "foreign-born agitator." In a letter published by the *New York Times*, Einstein spoke out against government intimidation through HUAC.

"What ought the minority of intellectuals to do against this evil?" he asked. "Frankly, I can see only the revolutionary way of noncooperation in the sense of Gandhi's. Every intellectual who is called before one of the committees ought to refuse to testify, i.e., he must be prepared for jail and economic ruin, in short, for the sacrifice of his personal welfare in the interest of the cultural welfare of his country . . . . If enough people are ready to take this grave step they will be successful. If not, then the intellectuals of this country deserve nothing better than the slavery . . . intended for them."

Although most of the press supported HUAC, liberal papers did not. "The most un-American activity in the United States today is the conduct of the congressional committee on un-American activities," declared the Detroit *Free Press.*

"The beliefs of men and women . . . [are] nobody's business but their own as the Bill of Rights mentions," editorialized the *New York Times.* "Neither Mr. Thomas nor the Congress is empowered to dictate what Americans shall think."

After a period of relative dormancy, HUAC came to life again in the Sixties to attack the rising anti-war Resistance. But witnesses now appearing before HUAC resisted in a new way. Instead of taking the Fifth Amendment and refusing to answer the Committee's questions, they avoided contempt citations by replying with devastating countercharges.

"Overnight a new kind of witness was born," observed a *Nation* article in 1966, "the witness who boils over with talk, who pleads no privilege and fills the record with his views and objections . . . . His testimony attacks the committee, its premises . . . bitingly, humorously, solemnly and fearlessly."

The Yippies introduced a comic element of revolutionary theater into Committee hearings. In response to his subpoena, Abby Hoffman appeared dressed in an American flag. Jerry Rubin showed up costumed as a solder of the Revolutionary War. His plan, he revealed later with a grin, was to "ridicule the whole thing because even they can't take themselves seriously if you're sitting there in some outlandish costume."

He protested so noisily at not being allowed to testify that he was arrested for disturbing the peace. Returning at a future date, he was barred from the hearing room because this time he arrived dressed as Santa Claus.

Dave Dellinger, Rennie Davis and Tom Hayden—all about to be indicted as members of the Chicago Seven—exploited their appearances before HUAC as a forum for their views. The dismayed Committee found it impossible to stop them.

"I did receive a subpoena, and I considered not coming," Dellinger testified, "because I think that one does not have to obey illegal and immoral orders. However, since I am anxious to tell everything that I know . . . and since I consider the Committee highly ineffective, I am perfectly happy to be here."

Tom Hayden told HUAC's Southern chairman, "I consider myself an organizer of a movement to put you and your Committee out of power, because I think you represent racist philosophy that has no meaning any more in the twentieth century . . . . Working in the South brought us face to face for the first time with the realities of the police state. Civil rights workers were arrested by the thousands, beaten by the hundreds, killed on one occasion, and terrorized by the police constantly."

Accused of encouraging Army desertions, Rennie Davis replied that he only encouraged servicemen "to feel that you do not have to give up your soul, your life, your beliefs because a sergeant yells at you to fall in or fall out . . . to understand that your body may be given to Uncle Sam, but not necessarily your mind, that as an American citizen you have certain rights, even within the military, to say that this [Vietnam] war is immoral and unjust, that you feel you have to somehow be heard on whether or not you will be forced to commit acts of genocide against another people."

Davis called for rebuilding the nation "to make this country something other than the people's policeman of the world." Asked whether he proposed to do it peacefully, he replied, "It depends on you. This Committee, this Congress, and this Government generally is so unrespon-

sive to what people are saying in this country, particularly
the young, that it becomes more and more difficult for us
to find any channel through which we can operate . . . .
It is people like you that are destroying America . . . . the
hope of America is in the people who will stand up to
people like you."

Such biting resistance discredited HUAC to such a
degree that soon afterward it had to be reorganized under
a new identity—the House Internal Security Committee.

Another form of government intimidation was the re-
quirement of loyalty oaths. A West Coast lawyer refused
to take one, explaining, "How do I know what our
government might be ten years from now? If it turned into
a dictatorship, I would reserve my right to revolt against
it."

Supreme Court Justice William O. Douglas supported
Americans who resisted signing anti-Communist oaths required for government employment: "Those who refuse to
take such an oath are often eminent people who . . .
could truthfully sign it . . . . [But they] do not believe that
a teacher or employee should be singled out and made to
forswear a course of past conduct."

The Nixon Administration used various tactics to intimidate the press and television into suppressing news unfavorable to the government and playing up Administration
statements. In biting attacks on the media, Vice President
Agnew accused them of an unfair liberal bias. Clay T.
Whitehead, director of the Office of Telecommunications
Policy, implied a threat to the license renewals of local
TV stations if they did not pressure the networks to
present more "balanced" news programs.

The government also sought to harass news reporters
who broke stories on government corruption by insisting
that they must reveal all their confidential sources to a
grand jury. Newsmen resisted such orders because betraying their sources would dry up future tips on
government wrongdoers, which often came from within
government departments.

To protect the public's "right to know," Peter Bridge, a *Newark Evening News* reporter, went to jail in October, 1972, for an indefinite period, rather than obey a court order to reveal his sources for news exposing corrupt officials.

Former NBC newscaster Sandy Vanocur charged that the Nixon Administration was "the most hostile toward the news media in White House history." He said, "The Nixon Administration would like to have people believe it's in bad taste to criticize the President . . . That's not what this country is about."

The government cut off funds for controversial programs on the Public Television network. And in March, 1973, CBS canceled the broadcast of a prize-winning anti-war play for fear of government reprisals. The Vietnam Veterans Against the War wrote an open letter of protest to CBS denouncing the cancellation as "obscene." They also protested the hours of coverage the TV networks devoted to the Administration theme that returning prisoners of war were American heroes.

"In actuality," they declared, "the majority of the POWs are career oriented professionals who voluntarily bombed schools and hospitals." Speaking for anti-war veterans, they added, "You can punish us, by not employing us; by sticking us in overcrowded, filthy hospitals; by cutting funds for our education; by beating our artificial limbs into new bombs; by keeping us out of your sight and hearing. But as long as we're alive, you'll have to face what we did, for we did it in your name."

When the unprecedented Watergate scandal began to break in 1973, involving the entire White House and its staff in illegal wire-tapping, burglaries, break-ins, blackmail, bribery, forgery, violations of the Bill of Rights and election laws, and cover-ups of crimes, the Nixon Administration desperately tried to suppress the disclosures. Government spokesmen denounced the *Washington Post* particularly for its "lies."

Resisting every pressure put upon them, the *Post's* editors doggedly kept up their investigation until the conspirators began confessing, rocking the nation with the whole sordid story. The President was forced to fire almost his whole staff and go on television to plead that he had not known what was going on. He now lauded the role of a "vigorous free press" in exposing the Watergate scandal and meekly told reporters to "give me hell every time I'm wrong."

His press secretary Ron Ziegler apologized to *Washington Post* reporters for having attacked them, and Vice President Agnew also apologized for his campaigns against the press. The *Washington Post* won the Pulitzer Prize for its notable achievement.

"Freedom of the press must be maintained . . . because it is the only way we have to discover truth and expose error," observed historian Henry Steele Commager. " . . . . Without a constant flow of criticism, a constant agitation of controversial questions, a constant expression of new and unfamiliar ideas, we are sure to make mistakes."

Thomas Jefferson once declared, "Were it left to me to decide whether we should have a government without newspapers, or newspapers without a government, I should not hesitate a moment to prefer the latter."

But despite the triumph of the truth in the Watergate scandal, normally individuals who resist the power of the Establishment must expect to pay the price that the majority, which supports the Establishment, extracts from any courageous minority which does not.

Once Danish critic Georg Brandes upset the faculty of Copenhagen University, where he taught literature, by his attacks on the powerful orthodox clergy. He complained to Henrik Ibsen that, as a result, he was ostracized, denied promotions and attacked bitterly in the Copenhagen press.

"You say that every voice in the faculty of philosophy is against you," Ibsen replied. "Dear Brandes, how else would you want it? Are you not fighting against the philosophy of the faculty? You cannot fight your war as a paid employee of the King. If they did not lock you out, it would show that they were not afraid of you."

A government driven to suppress its Resistance acts out of fear. Such fear is often greatest when those in the Resistance prove that they themselves do not fear the consequences of their opposition, and are willing to pay that price for the right to carry the truth to the people. Daniel Ellsberg demonstrated just such courage when he invited arrest and trial by publishing the secret Pentagon Papers that exposed government lies to the public about the Vietnam War.

17 You, Me and
the Government

The Nixon Administration, enlarging the war in Vietnam during the President's first administration, was worried by increasingly defiant anti-war demonstrations. The President warned students, "We have the power to strike back if need be, and to prevail. The nation has survived other attempts at insurrection. We can survive this."

In May, 1969, U.S. Deputy Attorney General Richard Kleindienst, who later resigned in the Watergate scandal, threatened, "If people demonstrate in a manner to interfere with others, they should be rounded up and put in a detention camp."

But former U.S. Attorney General Ramsey Clark warned, "Repressiveness is the worst kind of police-community relations possible. No one likes to be pushed around, to be denied his rights, and few will readily forget or forgive it. Police brutality, sweep arrests, roundups of people when there is no probable cause to believe they committed a criminal act, and the unnecessary use of deadly force—these embitter beyond all other acts."

Resistance movements are based on the principle that not all law is good law or sound law. When citizens consider a law bad, they have the right to resist it to force its testing in the Supreme Court. Some authorities believe that there should be no punishment at all for acts which clearly intend to do just that. The President's Commission on Law Enforcement held that civil disobedience is not criminal disobedience.

The government itself may have committed a crime by sending draft resisters to jail for five years for burning their draft cards. Respect for the law must come from respectable laws, some legal experts insist, not from punishing those who resist laws unworthy of respect.

"A legal order, no less than a parent, must earn and deserve the respect of its constituents," states Professor of Law Joseph L. Sax of the University of Michigan, "it must legitimate itself . . . by aspiring toward justice."

What happens when the legality of a law that officials attempt to enforce is in dispute? Professor Pauline Maier, in her book *From Resistance to Revolution*, notes that colonial governments were careful about using violence against resistance. "Since turbulence indicated above all some shortcoming in government," she points out, "it was never to be met by increasing the authorities' power of suppression."

One colonist wrote in 1768, "The only effectual way to prevent uprisings is to govern with wisdom, justice and moderation."

Perhaps jail sentences should be only nominal, or suspended, for those who resist a law to challenge it as unjust or unconstitutional. Justification for such leniency can be found in the protection of protest and civil disobedience under the First Amendment.

"Men in authority will always think that criticism of their policies is dangerous," observes historian Henry Steele Commager. "They will always equate their policies with patriotism and find criticism subversive. The Federalists found criticism of President Adams so subversive that they legislated to expel critics from the country. Southerners found criticism of slavery so subversive that they drove critics out of the South . . . . Mc-

Carthy found almost all teachers and writers so subversive that he was ready to burn down the libraries and close the universities. Experience should harden us against the argument that dissent and criticism are so dangerous that they must always give way to concensus."

The New Hampshire state constitution declares, "Whenever the ends of government are perverted and public liberty manifestly endangered and all other means of redress are ineffectual, the people may, and of right ought to, reform the old or establish a new government. The doctrine of nonresistance against arbitrary power and oppression is absurd, slavish, and destructive of the good and happiness of mankind."

"God forbid we should be twenty years without a rebellion," wrote Thomas Jefferson in 1787. "What country can preserve its liberties if the rulers are not warned from time to time that their people preserve the spirit of resistance?"

When Jefferson succeeded Adams as President, he threw out Adams' Alien and Sedition Laws, considering them illegal.

"I discharged every person under punishment or prosecution under the sedition law," he explained, "because I considered and now consider, that law to be a nullity, as absolute and as palpable as if Congress had ordered us to fall down and worship a golden image; and that it was as much my duty to arrest its execution at every stage, as it would have been to have rescued from the fiery furnace those who should have been cast into it for refusing to worship the image. It was accordingly done in every instance, without asking what the offenders had done, or against whom they had offended, but whether the pains they were suffering were inflicted under the pretended sedition law."

No new Jefferson has yet appeared to rescue from jail or exile those punished for resisting the Vietnam War. Many were among the nation's best-educated and most highly principled young people, who paid a heavy penalty for resisting a war before the majority of Americans was finally convinced that they were right about it. Yet it was their resistance that led the majority to change its mind at last and demand an end to American involvement in Vietnam.

Change is essential in any nation if it is not to stagnate. New ways must be found to legalize civil disobedience and keep it nonviolent. "A legitimate government should be able to find some way of extending its understanding, its intelligence, its reason, and its tolerance to the revolutionary process," suggested Dean Scott Buchanan of St. John's College. He added, "It would be a great thing if we could discover what it is that would bring revolution in as a legitimate process."

President Nixon paid lip service to that idea when he addressed Congress in January, 1971. "What this Congress can be remembered for is opening the way to a new American Revolution," he declared, "a peaceful revolution in which power was turned back to the people—in which government at all levels was refreshed and renewed, and made truly responsive. This can be a revolution as profound, as far-reaching, and as exciting as that first revolution almost two hundred years ago."

The Roosevelt Administration found a way of legitimatizing resistance and civil disobedience. During the early part of the century, labor unions frequently resorted to illegal actions to fight oppressive practises by big business. The courts were on the side of the corporations; strikes and strike tactics were often held unlawful. When the New Deal passed the Wagner Labor Relations Act, it legitimatized labor's resistance tactics. Today we consider strikes and strike tactics perfectly legal. Ironically, labor leaders, once branded flaming revolutionaries, are considered today's ultraconservatives.

In many cities police are now learning how to handle demonstrations with a minimum use of force and a maximum exercise of tact. To the extent that they refrain from inflicting violence on protesters, protesters will in turn remain largely nonviolent. It is to be hoped that the country has seen its last students, blacks or innocent bystanders clubbed down or shot during demonstrations. "Who will protect the public," asked Ramsey Clark, "when the police violate the law?"

Interestingly enough, President Nixon himself openly violated the law in July, 1973, when he refused to turn over secretly-recorded White House tapes as ordered by both a grand jury subpoena and two subpoenas from The Senate's Watergate investigation committee. The President resisted the law because he considered it unconstitutional, and he sought a ruling from the Supreme Court.

Americans who most need the protection of the Bill of Rights are the poor or powerless; the advocates of unorthodox ideas; those who belong to minority religious, racial, political or cultural groups; and opponents of the power structure. The Bill of Rights gives the Davids of America one slingshot to use against the Goliath that controls the nation's major institutions—the right to resist.

President Franklin D. Roosevelt recognized the value of protest demonstrations to our society. Once a delegation came to see him demanding his support for a badly-needed reform measure. When the delegates had finished arguing their case, the President nodded and declared, "Okay, you've convinced me. *Now go on out and bring pressure on me!*"

18 Resistance
Brings Change

Small triumphs, one after the other, add up to a changing America—slowly but inevitably. Resistance forces change where otherwise none would come. It also speeds up changes that would otherwise come at a snail's pace.

In 1972, when Jane Fonda and Tom Hayden sought to hold a peace rally to report on their trip to North Vietnam, the city of Kingston, New York, denied them a permit. The American Civil Liberties Union sued the city and won an injunction. The rally went on.

Four demonstrators with anti-war signs tried to picket Philadelphia's Convention Hall while President Nixon was speaking there but were arrested. Sueing the city, the ACLU compelled police to respect the right of Resistance groups to demonstrate in public areas anywhere in Philadelphia.

When his draft board rejected his claim to be a conscientious objector because he wasn't religious, Harvard graduate John Heffron Sisson, Jr., went to jail in 1968 for refusing induction. On appeal, a U.S. District judge declared the section of the draft law requiring COs to be religious unconstitutional. Subsequently as many as fourteen thousand young men a year were able to claim CO status because of deep moral convictions.

David Earl Gutknecht defied the draft by attending a Minneapolis anti-war rally in 1967 and throwing his draft card at the feet of a Federal marshal. His draft board classified him 1A as a "delinquent." Refusing induction, he was given a four-year jail term. He fought the case all the way up to the Supreme Court, which reversed his conviction and held illegal attempts by draft boards to intimidate war protesters by labeling them delinquents. Gutknecht's fight prevented thousands who joined the Resistance from being so punished.

At Fort Jackson in South Carolina, members of G.I.s United Against the War In Vietnam spoke against the war during off-duty hours. Placed under arrest, they filed suit in Federal court, demanding the same rights of dissent as civilians. The Army hastily decided to drop its charges against them.

When servicemen Kenneth W. Stolte, Jr., and Donald F. Amick distributed anti-war leaflets at Fort Ord, the Army sentenced them to three years' imprisonment for "disloyalty." They appealed to a U.S. District Court, which reversed their conviction and upheld their rights under the First Amendment. It was the first time in American history that a civilian court had ever overruled a military court-martial.

After the breakdown in Vietnam peace talks at the end of 1972, B-52 pilot Michael J. Heck balked at President Nixon's orders to resume bombing Hanoi. Having flown 175 missions, Heck refused to fly the 176th because "the goals do not justify the mass destruction and killing." The Air Force threatened him with a court-martial, but the ACLU intervened and demanded his release from the Air Force. The ACLU won.

"The unprecedented level of resistance to military service in recent years," observed social critic David Cortwright, "has caused basic changes in American military policy."

The Resistance compelled the Army to reform its whole system of military justice. In a memo to all commanding officers called *Guidance On Dissent,* the Secretary of the Army acknowledged the rights of servicemen to distribute political literature on military bases, to publish underground newspapers, to wear non-G.I. haircuts, to attend coffeehouses, and to join servicemen's unions. Such concessions would have seemed incredible to powerless draftees of previous eras.

The phasing out of the draft and Nixon's proposals for an all-volunteer army also signified victories for the Resistance. So did the realization by the majority of Americans that the Vietnam War was wrong and ought to end as quickly as possible with a peace settlement, not an attempt at victory.

Successes of the anti-war movement inspired other groups to use resistance tactics to achieve their own objectives.

Police who were refused pay raises began enforcing traffic regulations overzealously, upsetting taxpayers with a flood of tickets. Conservationists sought to stop developers from putting up high-rise apartments in country areas by interposing their own bodies in front of the bulldozers. Welfare clients, Indians and other minority groups staged sit-ins at government bureaus to protest unfair treatment.

Women's Lib won an impressive string of victories by its resistance. Military academies were forced to admit women. The Navy agreed to let women go to sea. Female athletic coaches won equal pay with male coaches. Pregnant students won the right to attend graduation ceremonies. Police and fire departments eliminated requirements that kept women from applying. Women were allowed to vote using their maiden names. And the Supreme Court upheld women's right to legal abortions, no small victory over the opposition of President Nixon.

Although the Nixon Administration moved America more conservatively to the Right on domestic matters, the Resistance was still able to press ahead with gains. "If a minority is sufficiently well-organized and skillful in its resistance," noted the ACLU's Ira Glasser in 1973, "it can have a disproportionate impact. Liberty can still be protected."

A case in point was Harvard Professor Samuel Popkin, who was jailed for refusing to reveal the sources of his knowledge about publication of the Pentagon Papers. When Harvard and the American Association of University Professors protested indignantly, he was suddenly released after a week behind bars.

Fed up with the squalor of New York ghettos, minority groups won action on their grievances by civil disobedience.

"In the Bronx," related Mayor John Lindsay, "protests against dirty streets became troublesome when residents began setting fire to garbage in the street. The police precinct commander and the task force leader immediately brought a sanitation truck to the area to remove the garbage, which eased tempers . . . . Police could have arrested the dissidents—peacefully or forcefully. But the police . . . recognized that these acts were not crimes and that a mechanism existed that might restore order more quickly and at much less cost."

The Sixties saw great strides in establishing the dignity of American blacks through Resistance tactics. In one historic case Mary Hamilton, a black defendant, refused to answer an Alabama district attorney when he patronizingly called her "Mary." The court sentenced her to jail for contempt. The ACLU helped her fight the case up to the Supreme Court, which set her free.

"The black revolt and the white response of the '50s and '60s produced enormous progress—more than in the three-quarters of a century since Reconstruction," observed *Newsweek* magazine. "The legal structure of Jim Crow in the South was brought down. The segregation of public schools by law was effectively ended. The Voting Rights Act of 1965 enfranchised two million new black voters and helped elect hundreds of Southern blacks to public office, from county commissioner to congressman.

Expanding economic opportunities nourished the development of a large, growing and increasingly visible black middle class."

That middle class had grown from only five percent to one third of all black families in just thirty years.

Conservationists also used resistance tactics to advantage. Their agitation against pollution forced government and industry alike to alter "business as usual" policies and begin offering plans to clean up America's air and water.

The government was forced to create an Environmental Agency, which ordered Detroit manufacturers to install pollution control devices on new cars made from 1976 on. Factories were forbidden to dump raw sewage in lakes and rivers. Farmers were stopped from using fish- and bird-killing pesticides.

President Nixon and Prime Minister Pierre Trudeau of Canada signed a treaty for a massive two-nation program to clean up the Great Lakes. Lumber companies were forced to observe conservation precautions in cutting timber. Many states began stricter supervision of mining companies to see that they relandscaped lands gouged by huge earthmoving machinery.

Resistance also brought striking changes in the whole life style of the country. When young people balked at short hair, "square" music, staid clothes and "proper" speech, they started a cultural revolution that spread rapidly across the generations. They led many Americans to begin seeking a more meaningful life style through communes, country living, arts and crafts, and rock festivals. Rejecting the older generation's favorite drug, alcohol, some young people caused an uproar by experimenting with different drugs, primarily marijuana.

The spirit of resistance penetrated even the most conservative rural regions. In upstate New York, Colleen Di-Micco was ordered to leave a Rhinebeck restaurant because she was not wearing a bra. She filed a complaint with the Human Rights Division, charging discrimination since men were not told what undergarments they must wear. The Division compelled the restaurant owner to apologize and readmit Miss DiMicco, along with all other women who chose not to wear bras.

Similarly Michael Braun, refused service at a Tonawanda, New York, restaurant for wearing long hair, brought suit because long-haired women were served. A State Supreme Court judge upheld his charge of sex discrimination and ordered the restaurateur to admit and serve all long-haired customers.

A one-inch beard worn by Peter Connelly, an Erie County, New York, Jail employee, offended the sheriff, who ordered him to shave it off. He refused and was fired. A State Supreme Court judge ordered him reinstated with both full pay and beard.

A significant victory for all youthful resisters occurred in November, 1971, when eighteen-year-olds, for the first time in American history, won the right to vote in elections. Two nineteen-year-old college students won elections as mayors.

When law student Paul Soglin took part in a 1969 peace demonstration in Madison, Wisconsin, he was arrested by the police force of conservative Mayor William Dyke, and his shaggy long hair was forcibly shaved off. Four years later, he organized a coalition of liberals, students, antiwar activists, minorities and labor groups. Running against Dyke for Mayor, Soglin won and dumped the chagrined official out of office.

The Resistance could point with pride to compelling the Democratic Party to reform its election primaries, opening its ranks in 1972 to full participation by youths, women and ethnic minorities. For the first time in American history a woman was named "chairperson" of the Democratic Party.

If the Resistance did not succeed in completely overhauling the Establishment, its scattered victories helped to introduce an experimental mood in which the idea of change became acceptable and desirable. University operations today are certainly different because of the student Resistance, and universities now take student views into consideration in making decisions.

Underground newspapers have forced a loosening of rigid censorship that not long ago was almost Victorian in dictating what could be said aloud or in print. Demonstrators have definitely stretched the former limits of protest.

When the University of Wisconsin banned the use of loudspeakers on campus during the Vietnam War Moratorium, students defied the order and were arrested. Federal District Judge James E. Doyle declared the ban illegal, violating constitutional guarantees of free speech. "Freedom of assembly and expression is to be honored no less for political purposes," he ruled, "than for . . . Homecoming and Campus Carnival."

Thanks to the ACLU, many teachers fired for resistance activities won reinstatement with back pay. One had been dismissed for designing a classroom Christmas display that had included a poster reading: "War is Not Healthy for Children and Other Living Things." Teachers fired for refusing to sign a New York State loyalty oath were ordered reinstated by the U.S. Supreme Court.

Resistance, said Representative Shirley Chisholm, must be kept up continually and relentlessly. Otherwise, she warned, "The beneficiaries of the system will never change the status quo."

Discouraged young Americans often ask themselves, "But what can *we* do about changing so many things that are wrong?"

One can do what is within one's power—joining others with the same beliefs who resist personally, as best they can, in every way they can, as peacefully as they can, injustices of the Establishment that offend human conscience. Small, determined groups can have tremendous impact.

After the Second World War nuclear power was still under military control. A handful of American scientists grew alarmed at the power of the Pentagon to trigger a world holocaust. Armed with little more than a mimeograph machine, they protested vehemently. Their alarm galvanized the scientific community into bringing intense pressure to bear on Congress, which transferred the development of atomic energy to civilian control.

Resisting the will of the various powerful majorities that make up the Establishment is never easy. But with determination, courage and persistence, a resistance movement with a just cause can compel them to make necessary changes.

"I think it is undeniable," declared Hannah Arendt in a *New Yorker* article on civil disobedience, "that these majorities have changed in mood and opinion to an astounding degree under the pressure of the minorities."

The secret is to act where you have power.

19 Act Where You Have Power

Democracy is built upon government by majority, requiring orderly laws applicable to all. But dissent is essential for change in human affairs. If there had been no dissent since our nation was founded, we would still be using only laws designed for the world of the 1770s to cope with the complex problems of the 1970s. If dissent did not produce change, moreover, the nation would become increasingly polarized between those who wanted change and those who did not, until only a violent revolution could resolve the conflict.

Revolt by the individual against what is wrong in society is therefore an exercise in good citizenship, necessary if our society is to improve, survive and thrive. "Revolt is necessary," said Supreme Court Justice Douglas, "if we are to avoid becoming a second-class nation."

Resistance becomes increasingly difficult, however, as the media fall increasingly into fewer and fewer hands, restricting the opportunities for dissenters to present their case adequately to the public.

Voting against candidates, parties and programs they oppose is a legal form of resistance available to all citizens. "Turning the rascals out" on Election Day is a time-honored form of peaceful revolution. But the Establishment has resources of power, money and access to the media enormously superior to those of the Resistance and can easily influence vastly more voters.

Inflation is a case in point. After World War II the government, under pressure from big business, removed all price controls. A tiny consumer resistance movement warned that this would only lead to spiraling prices and inflation, and it did, year after year. But the Resistance could not make its tiny voice heard against government propaganda in all the media labeling price controls Communistic and ruinous to the economy. It took twenty-seven years for the public to become so oppressed by inflation that mass resistance finally compelled the government to reapply price controls.

When the institutions of society seem too distant, too unreachable and unresponsive, the individual can only act where he has power to compel change. For most young people that means in the home, in the school, in the church, in local organizations, in the neighborhood. To win a voice in decision-making, they need to join with other like-minded youth in pressing together to win redress of their grievances. Nonviolent protests, and civil disobedience when justified, are legitimate tactics.

It is no coincidence that youth was in the forefront of the civil rights and anti-war movements. Young people are always the most idealistic and energetic of the generations, and it is their future that is at stake. It is largely up to youth to reshape the world of tomorrow to make it a better place for all to live in than previous generations have made it.

Youth has learned to be skeptical of election campaign promises. Some candidates do try to keep them. But many depend on election funds contributed by special interests which oppose change in the direction of greater democracy. Constructive change usually comes only after resistance groups organize strong pressure upon legislators anxious to be reelected.

Violence is rarely the best tactic. It may win attention, but in most cases people are turned against those who initiate violence, no matter how just their cause. Aware of this, the Establishment has often planted agents provocateur within resistance movements to goad dissenters into violent acts that will discredit them in the public eye. These agents even supply guns and explosives. Violence may shock people into awareness of a social problem, but in terms of winning their support it is usually counterproductive.

Seasoned veterans of resistance movements try to keep anarchists from seizing control. Anarchists are out not for reform but for a complete overturn of the system, no matter how bloody a revolution it takes. They urge violence knowing that it will provoke counterviolence from police and troops, which they hope will radicalize millions. What usually happens instead, however, is a government crackdown on all dissidents, peaceful as well as violent, and a setback to all progress.

In over two centuries, anarchistic tactics in America have failed to bring about a second violent revolution. The most significant changes, instead, have come about through persistent and peaceful civil disobedience.

"The most 'militant' actions of recent years," points out thrice-arrested Reverend Richard John Neuhaus of Brooklyn, New York, "have often been undertaken by those who are ideologically nonviolent . . . . [Even] before the Vietnam war was an issue, pacifists sailed into nuclear testing zones, tied up munitions factories, organized tax resistance groups and obstructed congressional hearings with sit-ins and counter-spectacles."

Resisting injustice can be a lonely and uncomfortable experience without the support of mass demonstrations. It is not easy to insist upon independence of thought under pressures from the majority to conform, to accept the status quo, to "go along to get along," as freshmen Senators are advised. In a roomful of one's peers, it takes raw courage to stand up alone and be counted in resistance.

Inspiration for such courage comes from the examples of other brave figures who steeled themselves for the ordeal. Jesus. Gandhi. Thoreau. Martin Luther King. The freedom riders. The draft card burners. The defiers of dictators.

It is a mistake to underestimate the power of a single figure with the courage to challenge the majority he believes to be wrong. Ibsen reminded us that the majority of today was the minority of twenty years ago; it takes that long for popular opinion to catch up with advanced ideas.

"Every new opinion, at its starting," agreed Thomas Carlyle, "is precisely in a minority of one."

Writing in *Walden*, Thoreau had advice for youth dissatisfied with the Old Order: "What old people say you cannot do, you try and find that you can. Old deeds for old people, and new deeds for new."

Tom Paine, who inspired Americans with the determination to defy British tyranny in 1776, suggested how one found the courage to resist: "The strength and powers of despotism consist wholly in the fear of resisting it . . . . In order *'to be free it is sufficient that he wills it.'* "

The resistance of just one courageous man can have a profound effect upon a whole nation. In 1925, Tennessee forbade the teaching of evolution because it contradicted the Biblical legend of the creation. The ACLU offered to defend any teacher arrested for resisting this law. John Scopes of Dayton High School volunteered, broke the law and was indicted.

Clarence Darrow defended him so brilliantly against prosecutor William Jennings Bryan, former Secretary of State, that only one other state ever passed an anti-evolution law. Science teachers all over America thus won the right to teach the knowledge of a world-wide galaxy of scholars and scientists.

Young people have opportunities to make a stand for freedom in many of their daily life activities, including school, work, recreation, civic participation, relations with parents and church, and membership in an ecology group.

No social institutions are ever perfectly managed. A person who sees new ways to make them operate more democratically can not only make a valuable contribution to society by opposing faulty old ways but also gain training in reshaping the world he will occupy tomorrow.

In an address at Princeton, New York's Mayor John Lindsay compared the frustrations of high school and college students with those of ghetto minorities. All three groups, he pointed out, "suffer the malady of power-lessness—powerlessness in the face of huge, authoritarian institutions that routinely cause fundamental dislocations in the lives of the people they affect each day."

In 1970 a resistance movement of New York City high school students formed a City General Organization Council, representing 275,000 students who demanded student participation in their education. The Council called for representative student government in each school, "free from domination by the administration and faculty adviser," with the right to act on all matters affecting students. It also demanded freedom of expression anywhere in the school, without penalty.

The Council's president, seventeen-year-old Donald St. George Reeves, was suspended for protesting school budget cuts. He was reinstated next day when several hundred students demonstrated in his support. "You're always caught in the middle when you try to accomplish something instead of talking," he declared. "But then, nobody ever said it was easy."

The law varies from state to state in its rulings on school dress and grooming codes. But court rulings have been handed down in favor of students who were punished for resisting regulations forbidding mustaches, beards, "extreme style and fashion," slacks for girls and skull caps.

"Certainly the school would be the first to concede that in a society as advanced as that in which we live there is room for many personal preferences," ruled Judge W. G. Watson of the California Superior Court, "and great care should be exercised insuring that what are mere personal preferences of one are not forced upon another for mere convenience, since absolute uniformity among our citizens should be our last desire."

The U.S. Supreme Court has held that "students in school as well as out of school are 'persons' under our constitution . . [and] possessed of fundamental rights which the state must respect." Students have a right to follow their conscience in resisting regulations abhorrent to their principles.

A West Virginia student was punished for refusing to salute the flag because the Pledge offended his religious scruples against offering obedience to any authority but God. The Court ruled that it was unconstitutional for him to be compelled to do so, because the free exercise of a person's religious beliefs must be removed "from all official control."

The student Resistance of the 1960s forced change in the regulations of New York City's school system. In late 1969 the city's Board of Education recognized the right of high school students to practice peaceful dissent and to have a voice in school matters that concern them. The Board also eased censorship of school newspapers, permitted the distribution of Resistance literature, and allowed students to wear civil rights or anti-war insignia on their clothes.

In 1966 a U.S. Court of Appeals upheld the right of Mississippi high school students to wear "freedom buttons" in school "as a means of silently communicating an idea." In 1969 the U.S. Supreme Court upheld the right of Iowa students to wear anti-war armbands to school, ruling, "Students are entitled to freedom of expression of their views."

In the view of the ACLU, students and student organizations must be allowed to hold meetings in school rooms or auditoriums, or on school grounds, to discuss freely, and pass resolutions about, any matter concerning them. They should also be allowed to demonstrate, picket or march peacefully as long as they do not disrupt classes or other school activities, although the ACLU considers it advisable to give advance notice to the authorities to avoid conflicts of any kind.

Student editor Peter Hodes of New York City's Charles Evans Hughes High School wrote an editorial criticizing the school's teachers and administrators. The principal, who saw it before it was printed, ordered it deleted from the paper. Hodes resisted by printing it in handbills and distributing them.

When the principal fired him as editor, almost every student on the paper resigned in protest. Determined upon his right to freedom of the press, Peter Hodes went to court. A judge ruled that his constitutional rights had been violated by punishing him for distributing handbills outside the school, thus compelling his reinstatement as editor.

The resistance of high school editors to censorship has been a frequent source of controversy. In 1972 the ACLU won a decision from the New York State Board of Education prohibiting the state's eight hundred school boards from limiting or restricting the content of any student publication, unless they can show that "substantial disruption or material interference with school activities" would result.

The New York Civil Liberties Union put out a Student Rights Handbook to acquaint students with their rights as citizens. When a group of students sought to distribute copies, school authorities forbade them. Supported by the NYCLU, the students compelled the authorities to back down.

Students have also won the right to distribute political campaign literature at high schools; to collect signatures on petitions; to distribute questionnaires soliciting opinions on politics, clothes, music, drugs, television programs and sex; to demand and receive diplomas denied them for "failures in citizenship" because of resistance

activities; to resist exclusion from graduation exercises
for disciplinary reasons; to have their parents shown all
their school records; to receive student loans under the
National Defense Education Act even while protesting the
Vietnam War, draft boards and the ROTC.

Many high school students, frustrated at being treated
like second-class citizens simply because they are young
and powerless, have discovered to their amazement that
the Bill of Rights protects them, too.

Some have successfully fought suspensions made
without formal hearings of charges against them, as a violation of their civil liberties. Court decisions in a number
of states have upheld their right to such hearings. In one
1970 case, *Hobson v. Bailey*, a high school student won the
right to know the names of witnesses who had testified
against him and to present testimony and witnesses of his
own.

Some students have resisted attempts by school authorities or police to search their lockers, as a violation of
their rights under the Fourth Amendment. Some states
have upheld their resistance, while others have not, and
the problem has still to be resolved by a Supreme Court
decision.

"Constitutional law regarding student rights is now in a
rapid state of flux," the ACLU declared in April, 1970, adding, "It will be wise, therefore, in the near future not
only to keep one moistened finger on the pages of
precedent, but to keep another pointed toward the strong
winds of change."

Resistance purely for the sake of resistance, when no
just cause is involved, is an exercise in futility. It may succeed in letting off steam, but one can accomplish nothing
except possibly get oneself hurt or into unnecessary
trouble. Participation in a riot, even though a person
abstains from acts of violence committed by others around
him, is held by most courts to be an act of delinquency, not
of civil disobedience.

Resistance in defense of a just cause is a different matter. To recognize a just cause an American needs to be familiar with the Bill of Rights, the first ten amendments by the Founding Fathers who refused to adopt the Constitution until they were added. The Bill of Rights contains every citizen's guarantees of justice against oppression and repression.

When a person supports anyone who protests violation of his constitutional rights, his resistance upholds the Constitution on behalf of all Americans. Freedom is indivisible. If one person is denied his rights, everybody can be.

Free elections in an open society offer the only opportunity of change without violence and without scrapping every liberal institution in the process. But change is painfully slow without a determined resistance movement dedicated to ever greater freedom, ever greater justice, for the individual.

"What is really needed," declared Henrik Ibsen, "is a revolution of the human spirit." Such a revolution should begin with the self—resistance to all the unjust ideas implanted in one by majority concepts such as racial prejudice; contempt for the poor; indifference toward others' problems as long as one's self is not affected; hatred for those who think, act or dress differently; or arrogance toward people of other nations. These attitudes, privately or openly espoused by the majority, become the basis for an unjust society.

To resist majority pressures a person must have the courage to say no when everyone expects him to say yes, to refuse whether it involves refusing to smoke pot, to wave the flag, to snub minorities, to wear the latest fad, to scream at rock singers, to mock parents or to talk baseball. We should agree to only what we truly believe in—do our own thing. To do the majority's thing, while privately disliking it, is hypocritical.

Resistance tactics can be used to strengthen each of us in everyday life, changing—without destroying—those we disagree with. Common sense dictates first of all making every effort to resolve a conflict or redress a grievance through established channels before taking any further steps.

But if we cannot persuade a stubborn authority to listen, it may be necessary to escalate resistance to a second level—preparing a group of those who feel as we do for direct action. When an authority becomes aware that his persistence in an unfair regulation or law is provoking group resistance, he may rethink the issue and offer concessions.

The third step is public agitation—propaganda and such demonstrations as mass meetings, parades, slogan-shouting and other peaceful tactics to bring our grievances to public attention, and win popular support. The more imaginative the tactics, the more likely they are to win media coverage.

A beautiful example occurred in May, 1973, when the Nixon Administration slashed funds for public and school libraries, crippling their special services to the blind, the aged and the handicapped, while raising the military budget in peacetime to $85 billion. On signal from the American Library Association, every public library in the country dimmed its lights symbolically until the library fell dark, while air raid sirens warned the American people of the government's attack upon their halls of enlightenment. Such tactics are often upsetting and embarrassing to authorities and may lead to an offer to negotiate grievances.

The fourth step in escalating resistance is the announcement of an ultimatum. The group reveals its plan of a boycott or some act of nonviolent civil disobedience if no agreement is reached. At the same time the authorities are offered a constructive and reasonable settlement they cannot reject out of hand without appearing unreasonable in public opinion.

If none of these tactics produces movement toward change, the resistance group then has no alternative but to carry out the boycott or act of civil disobedience. If this action violates a regulation or the law, members of the group must be prepared to be punished accordingly for the courage of their convictions—suspension, firing or arrest. Unless they are, they had better limit resistance to the first three steps.

If their punishment is illegal or oversevere, however, the American Civil Liberties Union will fight for their rights before a court or board.

Resistance to tyranny made us a free nation in 1776. Resistance to tyranny over our minds, spirits and bodies will keep us a free people beyond 1984, the grim date in George Orwell's prophecy when we would become a regimented society.

Whether we remain free depends largely on the willingness of American youth to resist injustice. Only by the courage of their convictions can youth make the freedom-expanding minority of today the majority of tomorrow. We can take heart from Thoreau's credo, "Any man more right than his neighbors constitutes a majority of one already."

Bibliography and
Suggested Further Reading
(• Indicates Recommended Reading)

Adler, Renata. *Toward A Radical Middle.* New York: Random House, 1969.

Adler, Ruth. *The Working Press.* Toronto/New York/London: Bantam Books, Inc., 1970.

• Archer, Jules. *African Firebrand: Kenyatta of Kenya.* New York: Julian Messner. 1969.

• ——— *Chou En-lai.* New York: Hawthorn Books, Inc., Publishers, 1973.

• ——— *Congo: the Birth of a New Nation.* New York: Julian Messner, 1970.

• ——— *The Extremists: Gadflies of American Society.* New York: Hawthorn Books, Inc., Publishers, 1969.

• ——— *Famous Young Rebels.* New York: Julian Messner, 1973.

• ——— *Hawks, Doves, and the Eagle.* New York: Hawthorn Books, Inc., Publishers, 1970.

• ——— *Ho Chi Minh: Legend of Hanoi.* New York: Crowell-Collier Press, 1971.

• ——— *Indian Foe, Indian Friend.* New York: Crowell-Collier Press, 1970.

• ——— *Mao Tse-tung.* New York: Hawthorn Books, Inc., Publishers, 1972.

- ——— *1968: Year of Crisis.* New York: Julian Messner, 1971.
- ——— *The Philippines' Fight For Freedom.* New York: Crowell-Collier Press, 1970.
- ——— *Red Rebel: Tito of Yugoslavia.* New York: Julian Messner, 1968.
- ——— *Revolution In Our Time.* New York: Julian Messner, 1971.
- ——— *Strikes, Bombs & Bullets: Big Bill Haywood and the IWW.* New York: Julian Messner, 1972.
- ——— *They Made A Revolution: 1776.* New York, Toronto, London, Auckland, Sidney, Tokoyo: Scholastic Book Services, 1973.
- ——— *Thorn In Our Flesh: Castro's Cuba.* New York: Cowles Book Company, Inc., 1970.
- ——— *Treason In America: Disloyalty versus Dissent.* New York: Hawthorn Books, Inc., Publishers, 1971.
- ——— *The Unpopular Ones.* New York: Crowell-Collier-Press, 1968.
  Ayling, S.E. *Portraits of Power.* New York: Barnes & Noble, Inc., 1963.
- Beauvoir, Simone de. *Djamila Boupacha.* New York: The Macmillan Company, 1962.
- Becker, Howard S., ed. *Campus Power Struggle.* New Brunswick, N.J.: Aldine Publishing Company, 1970.
- Becket, James. *Barbarism In Greece.* New York: Walker and Company, 1970.
- Bentley, Eric, ed. *Thirty Years of Treason.* New York: The Viking Press, 1971.
- Berger, Peter L. and Richard John Neuhaus. *Movement and Revolution.* Garden City, New York: Doubleday & Company, Inc., 1970.
- Berrigan, Daniel. *The Trial of the Catonsville Nine.* Toronto/New York/London: Bantam Books, Inc., 1971.
- Bessie, Alvah. *Inquisition in Eden.* New York: The Macmillan Company, 1965.
  Black, Algernon. *The People and the Police.* New York, Toronto, London, Sydney: McGraw-Hill Book Company, 1968.

Blumberg, Abraham S., ed. *The Scales of Justice.* New Brunswick, N.J.: Aldine Publishing Company, 1970.

Bosch, Juan. *Pentagonism.* New York: Grove Press, Inc., 1968.

Boveri, Margret. *Treason in the Twentieth Century.* New York: G.P. Putnam's Sons, 1963.

• Brée, Germaine and George Bernauer, eds. *Defeat and Beyond.* New York: Pantheon Books, 1970.

• Broudy, Eric, Warren Halliburton and Laurence Swinburne. *They Had a Dream.* New York: Pyramid Books, 1969.

The Bulletin of the Atomic Scientists. *China After the Cultural Revolution.* New York: Random House, 1969.

Bulloch, John. *Akin to Treason.* London: Arthur Barker Ltd., 1966.

The Center for the Study of Democratic Institutions. *The Establishment and All That.* Santa Barbara, California, undated.

Chomsky, Noam. *At War With Asia.* New York: Pantheon Books, 1970.

• Clark, Ramsey. *Crime In America.* New York: Simon and Schuster, 1970.

Cleaver, Eldridge. *Post-Prison Writings and Speeches.* New York: Random House, 1969.

Coffin, Tristram. *Senator Fulbright.* New York: E.P. Dutton & Co., Inc., 1966.

• Commager, Henry Steele. *Freedom and Order.* Cleveland and New York: The World Publishing Company, 1966.

Cooley, John K. *East Wind Over Africa.* New York: Walker and Company, 1965.

Cooper, Chester L. *The Lost Crusade.* New York: Dodd, Mead & Company, 1970.

• Cowan, Lore. *Children of the Resistance.* New York: Meredith Press, 1969.

• Dorman, Michael. *Under 21: A Young People's Guide to Legal Rights.* New York: Dell Publishing Co., Inc., 1970.

- Douglas, William O. *The Right of the People.* New York: Pyramid Communications, Inc., 1972.
- Douglass, James W. *Resistance and Contemplation.* Garden City, New York: Doubleday & Company, Inc., 1972.
- Draper, Hal. *Berkeley: The New Student Revolt.* New York: Grove Press, Inc., 1965.

  Eisenberg, Dennis. *The Re-emergence of Fascism.* New York: A.S. Barnes and Company, 1967.
- Epstein, Jason. *The Great Conspiracy Trial.* New York: Random House, 1970.
- "Free" (Abby Hoffman). *Revolution For the Hell of It.* New York: The Dial Press, Inc., 1968.

  Garabedian, John H. and Orde Coombs. *Eastern Religions in the Electric Age.* New York: Workman Publishing Company, 1969.

  Gardiner, Robert. *A World of Peoples.* New York: Oxford University Press, 1966.
- Gardner, Fred. *The Unlawful Concert.* New York: The Viking Press, 1970.
- Gaylin, Willard, M.D. *In the Service of Their Country: War Resisters in Prison.* New York: Grosset & Dunlap, 1970.

  Gerber, Albert B. *The Life of Adolph Hitler.* Philadelphia, Pa.: Mercury Books, Inc., 1961.

  Ginzburg, Ralph and Warren Boroson, eds. *The Best of Fact.* New York: Avant-Garde Books, 1967.
- Gold, Robert S., ed. *The Rebel Culture.* New York: Dell Publishing Co., Inc., 1970.

  Goldman, Eric F. *The Tragedy of Lyndon Johnson.* London: Macdonald and Company (Publishers) Ltd., 1969.
- Grant, Joanne, ed. *Black Protest.* Greenwich, Conn.: Fawcett Publications, Inc., 1968.

  Gunther, John. *Inside Europe Today.* New York and London: Harper & Brothers, 1961.
- Hofstadter, Richard and Michael Wallace, eds. *American Violence.* New York: Random House, 1971.

- Hook, Sidney, ed. *The Essential Thomas Paine.* New York and Toronto: The New American Library, 1969.
- Hope, Marjorie. *Youth Against the World.* Boston, Toronto: Little, Brown and Company, 1970.

  Hyman, Sidney. *The Politics of Consensus.* New York: Random House, 1968.

  Johnson, Lyndon Baines. *The Vantage Point.* New York: Popular Library, 1971.

  Kenworthy, Leonard S. and Erma Ferrari. *Leaders of New Nations.* Garden City, New York: Doubleday & Company, Inc., 1968.

  Lasch, Christopher. *The New Radicalism in America.* New York; Random House, 1965.

  Lifton, Robert Jay, ed. *America and the Asian Revolutions.* New Brunswick, N.J.: Aldine Publishing Company, 1970.

  Lindsay, John V. *The City.* New York: New American Library, Inc., 1970.

  Lobenthal, Joseph S., Jr. *Power and Put-on: The Law in America.* New York: Outerbridge & Dienstfrey, 1970.
- Ludwig, Bernard. *Civil Rights and Civil Liberties.* New York: Washington Square Press, 1968.

  Lukas, J. Anthony. *The Barnyard Epithet and Other Obscenities.* New York, Evanston, and London: Harper & Row, Publishers, 1970.
- ——— *Don't Shoot—We Are Your Children!* New York: Dell Publishing Co., Inc., 1971.

  Malraux, Andre. *Anti-Memoirs.* New York, Chicago, San Francisco: Holt, Rinehart and Winston, 1968.
- March, Tony, ed. *Darkness Over Europe.* Chicago, New York, San Francisco: Rand McNally & Company, 1969.
- Markmann, Charles Lam. *The Noblest Cry: A History of the American Civil Liberties Union.* New York: St. Martin's Press, 1965.

  McCord, John H., ed. *With All Deliberate Speed: Civil Rights Theory and Reality.* Urbana, Chicago, London: University of Illinois Press, 1969.

Meyer, Karl E. *Senator Fulbright.* New York: Macfadden Books, 1964.

• Miles, Michael W. *The Radical Probe: The Logic of Student Rebellion.* New York: Atheneum, 1971.

• Miller, Michael V. and Susan Gilmore, eds. *Revolution at Berkeley.* New York: Dell Publishing Co., Inc., 1965.

Mitgang, Herbert, ed. *America at Random.* New York: Coward-McCann, Inc., 1968.

Moquin, Wayne and Charles Van Doren, eds. *A Documentary History of the Mexican Americans.* Toronto/New York/London: Bantam Books, 1972.

Myers, Gustavus. *History of Bigotry in the United States.* New York: Capricorn Books, 1960.

• Newfield, Jack. *A Prophetic Minority.* New York: The New American Library, Inc., 1967.

• New York Review of Books. *Trials of the Resistance.* New York: Random House, Inc., 1970.

Osborne, John. *The Nixon Watch.* New York: Liveright Publishing Corporation, 1970.

• Priaulx, Allan and Sanford J. Ungar. *The Almost Revolution: France—1968.* New York: Dell Publishing Co., Inc., 1969.

Pullen, John J. *Patriotism in America.* New York:American Heritage Press, 1971.

Radler, D.H. *El Gringo.* Philadelphia and New York: Chilton Company, 1962.

• Reich, Charles A. *The Greening of America.* New York: Random House, 1970.

Report of the National Advisory Commission on Civil Disorders. New York: E.P. Dutton & Co., Inc., 1968.

• Sandman, Peter M. *Students and the Law.* New York: Collier Books, 1969.

• Scholl, Inge. *Students Against Tyranny.* Middletown, Ct.: Wesleyan University Press.

Segal, Ronald. *The Race War.* Toronto, New York and London: Bantam Books, 1967.

Shirer, William L. *The Rise and Fall of the Third Reich.* Greenwich, Conn.: Fawcett Publications, Inc., 1963.

Shub, Anatole. *An Empire Loses Hope.* New York: W.W. Norton, Inc., 1970.

• Spender, Stephen. *The Year of the Young Rebels.* New York: Random House, 1969.

• Spock, Benjamin, M.D. *Decent and Indecent: Our Personal and Political Behavior.* New York: The McCall Publishing Co., 1970.

Sprinchorn, Evert. *Ibsen: Letters and Speeches.* New York: Hill and Wang, 1964.

• Stanford, Gene, ed. *Generation Rap.* New York: Dell Publishing Co., Inc., 1971.

Steffens, Lincoln. *Autobiography.* New York: Harcourt, Brace & World, Inc., 1958.

• Stein, David Lewis. *Living the Revolution: the Yippies in Chicago.* Indianopolis, New York: The Bobbs-Merrill Company, 1969.

• Stone, I.F. *The Killings at Kent State.* New York: Vintage Books, 1971.

——— *Polemics and Prophecies 1967-1970.* New York: Vintage Books, 1970.

Thayer, George. *The Farther Shores of Politics.* New York: Simon and Schuster, 1968.

Toppin, Edgar A. *A Biographical History of Blacks in America Since 1528.* New York: David McKay Company, Inc., 1969.

• Touraine, Alain. *The May Movement: Revolt and Reform.* New York: Random House, 1971.

Trythall, J.W.D. *El Caudillo.* New York: McGraw-Hill Book Company, 1970.

• Vercours. *The Battle of Silence.* New York, Chicago, San Francisco: Holt, Rinehart and Winston, 1967.

• Walker, Daniel. *Rights In Conflict.* New York: The New American Library, 1968.

• Wallerstein, Immanuel and Paul Starr, eds. *The University Crisis Reader: Confrontation and Counterattack.* New York: Random House, 1971.

- Williams, Roger Neville. *The New Exiles: American War Resisters in Canada.* New York: Liveright Publishers, 1971.
  Wills, Garry. *Nixon Agonistes.* Boston: Houghton Mifflin Company, 1970.
- *The Second Civil War.* New York: The New American Library, 1968.
- Zashin, Elliot M. *Civil Disobedience and Democracy.* New York: The Free Press, 1972.

Resistance leaflets and pamphlets were also consulted in the preparation of this book, in addition to issues of the following publications: *America, American Civil Liberties Union Annual Reports* (and pamphlets), *The Center Magazine, The Christian Century, Christianity and Crisis, Civil Liberties, Civil Liberties in New York, Lithopinion, The Nation, Newsweek, New York Post, The New York Times, The New Yorker, The New York Times Magazine, New Zealand News, Public Affairs Pamphlets, Public Citizen Report, Radical America, The Saturday Review, Society, Trans-action, TV Guide* and *Variety.*

Index